HOW TO WRITE STORIES THAT SELL

How To Write
Stories That Sell

EDWARD S. FOX

Boston

THE WRITER, INC.

Publishers

808.3
F 83

Copyright © 1961, 1969, by Edward S. Fox

Library of Congress Catalog Card Number: 61-6680

Printed in the United States of America

CONTENTS

HOW TO WRITE STORIES THAT SELL

1

HOW TO WORK PROFESSIONALLY

WHEN I WAS a fledgling writer, I thought I was the only one who ever made mistakes. In fact it gave me such an inferiority complex that I gave up writing nearly every day. Now after twenty-five years in the business, both as a writer and as a teacher of writing, I have found that I was not alone in my misery. Many beginners flounder around for years trying to learn technique and a professional approach to their writing. The purpose of this book is to help you cut down those years of floundering on technique. The purpose of this chapter is to help you acquire a professional approach to your work.

There are really only three ways to learn the technique of writing. One is to study it, just as you studied history or mathematics in high school or college. Study the articles in the writers' magazines. Get some textbooks and read them over a number of times, until you thoroughly understand what they are saying. A single reading is never enough.

What about correspondence courses? I can only say that there are some not-so-good ones, and some that are very good, some that really get down to the basic elements. Don't be impressed by the size of the advertisements of these courses, or their elaborate claims. Look instead at the qualifications of the teachers, and how long they've been in business. And what about college courses in writing? Here again it's difficult to pick the right one. With writing courses I would look at the teacher's qualifications and the record of his students. Have any of them made sales? I know of one course where over two hundred sales have been made by students to a variety of markets, ranging from the little magazines to the big national ones. But the teacher is also a working author, and he teaches his course on a practical rather than a theoretical basis.

The second way to learn technique is to study the works of established authors. If you want to write for the magazines, read and study the magazines. If you want to be an historical novelist, read and study historical novels. If you want to be a mystery story writer, soak yourself in mystery stories. Look for the points of technique you've learned from your textbooks and see how the different authors have handled them. If you should like a passage of dialogue or characterization, try typing it out and see how it looks on manuscript paper, just as you might have written it. Doing this somehow brings it into sharper focus. One warning: Do *not* study the classics. Styles in writing change from century to century. I seriously doubt if Dickens or Thackeray as new authors would be published today, even though they stand with the greats in literature.

The third way to learn technique is the best way of all. Write. There is no surer and quicker way to becoming a selling writer than to write. If, to start with, you want to write exercises on the points of technique you're studying, fine. It wouldn't hurt at all to do this for six months or so, or until you learn what a real story is and how to construct it. But write you should, and every day.

Writing habits

This brings us to the subject of writing habits. You might as well start off your career with good, rather than bad, habits. The first—and best—good habit you should acquire is the one mentioned above. Write every day. And at the same hours. Please, don't be a mood writer. There are excellent writers who have to wait to be in the "mood" before they can write, but they are few. When they are writing a story, most professionals work as regularly as a bank clerk. My hours have always been from 8:30 A.M. to 3 P.M., and any day that I wasn't in the mood for writing I still sat at my typewriter those six and a half hours. A couple of times early in my own career I gave in to those moodless days and went fishing and, in each case, a month later I was still fishing. Now I have to be at death's door before anything will keep me from my typewriter at 8:30 A.M., or take me from it before three in the afternoon. You can put it into one word—discipline. A writer has no boss to tell him what to do and what not to do. He has to tell himself.

It is well, in my opinion, to write in the same place each day. You become familiar with your surroundings, and those surroundings automatically set up in you an urge to get to work. A change each day is apt to keep a writer off balance. Of course, some writing jobs might keep you travelling constantly, and you'd have to learn to adapt yourself to change, but I'm talking about writing in the bedroom one day, the living room the next, the cellar the third, within the confines of your own house. I've always had trouble finding a suitable place to write. I can stand any kind of noise, except voices. If I hear my neighbors talking out in their back yards, I have to bend an ear to hear what they're saying, and so stops all production. I've written in cellars and in attics and in cow barns with cows and flies and rats running over my feet. I've written in the back seat of my car parked out in the woods somewhere. I've written with cotton and a special pair of earphones stuffed in and over my ears. The best writing place I ever had was a house I bought for myself and family on a river bank. I built a dock out into the river, and at the end of the dock built a "studio." It looked a little as though Chic Sale had been the architect, but it was peaceful and quiet. To make it private as well, I hinged a section of the dock, added a winch, and I had a drawbridge that came up at 8:30 A.M. and wasn't lowered again until 3 P.M.

One of the questions most frequently asked me is whether or not a writer should use a notebook. I never have. I always have relied on my memory. The trouble is, my memory is notoriously bad, so maybe I should have kept a notebook. At any rate, if I did I would use it for ideas only. Ideas for stories. Ideas for characters. A conflict. The reason for someone's unusual behavior. I would not sit on a park bench and fill my notebook with wordy descriptions of interesting looking people walking by. I would not fill it with descriptions of a scene, such as a sunset, or my neighbor's flower garden.

Another question frequently asked me is whether or not a writer should rely on his friends and relatives for criticism. The answer, in a loud shout, is, "No!" Would a doctor turn to his friends and relatives for help on an unfamiliar operation? Friends and relatives can't criticize, for the simple reason that they know nothing of technique. Rely on an editor, yes. Rely on a professional writer, yes. Rely on a critic, yes. But steer clear of friends, especially if you want to retain their friendship. A writer's ego is more fragile than an eggshell. It resents criticism, unless it has complete confidence in the competency of its source. You might kick your best friend in the shins for saying he didn't like your story, but would you kick Hemingway if he said it?

Now, here comes a "don't". *Don't* let rejection slips get you down. That's easy advice, but it's a hard thing to do in practice, I know. At one time I allowed myself to fall into that trap of all traps. I became a "mailman watcher." Our mailman usually came at eleven in the morning, and by ten I'd be standing out on the sidewalk watching for him. Since I usually had twenty or thirty stories going the rounds, a day never went by that I didn't get back one or more. And each one threw me for such a loop I could hardly go back to writing. Don't let this happen to you. You'll be a lot happier person if you take rejections in your stride and realize that they are a necessary evil to the process of growing to be a writer.

Agents and editors

Since I've mentioned sending out stories, I think this is a good time to bring up the subject of agents. Should you have an agent, and how do you go about getting one? The sad truth is that a good and reputable agent is hard to come by. Agents are businessmen, not teachers. Their livelihood comes from selling clients' stories, not teaching beginners how to write. They want to deal with professionals, not amateurs. You can't blame them, even though it is rough on you. If, in some way, you can manage to convince an agent that you have outstanding talent, he may take you on. If you can claim a professional writer as a friend and if he has enough faith in your ability, you might be able to talk him into introducing you to his agent. Those are your only chances, until you have proven yourself. Once you have made some sales your chances of interesting an agent are much better.

My first story (and some two hundred or so after that) were sold without benefit of agent, and the same thing is being done by other writers every day. Agents may be cool toward beginning writers but, believe me, editors are not. I haven't yet met an editor who wasn't eager to find, encourage, and help an up-and-coming writer. They are constantly on the look-out for new writers of promise. On the other hand, they can seem to be the most hard-hearted and calloused people in the world when they reward a writer time after time with nothing more than a cold and formal rejection slip. If that is happening to you, don't blame the editor. The trouble may be that you have not yet, in their eyes, reached the status of a "new writer of promise." The fault may be that you have not been writing long enough, or that you may have not bent your efforts in the right direction.

Let me interject here a simple statement. It takes perseverance to become a writer. I have a friend who wrote for twenty years before making his first sale; now he's a top-selling author. I have another friend with real talent who couldn't take the disappointments and gave up at the end of a few months. It all depends on how much drive you have, on how much you want to be a writer. If you don't have that drive, you might as well never start. Most writers *have* to write. They are compelled to. Unless they do, they are miserable. This is one of the hardest things in the world for the layman to understand. Most writers are dedicated to their work. If they weren't, they would be laying brick.

Preparing your manuscript

Next in acquiring the professional approach to writing comes the proper preparation of your script. For your final copy it is best to use a good grade of white paper of sixteen-pound weight. For first drafts, and for the carbon copy of your final, use yellow second sheets. You can buy these for a dollar or two for five hundred sheets. Aside from the cost, another reason for using yellow is that you can tell at a glance which is your carbon or rough draft.

In the upper left-hand corner of the first page type

your name and address. Put your title about a third of the way down the first page. Six or seven lines below the title, start your story. I usually leave an inch to an inch and a half margin on the left side of my page and about a half inch on the right side. Starting on the second page number all succeeding pages either in the center or over by the right-hand corner.

If you don't own a typewriter and are planning to buy one, be sure to buy one with pica, or large, type. Elite, or small, type is hard on an editor's eyes. Elite also does not give the proper illusion. The editor is not used to it and instinctively he fights it.

Where should you send your script when it is finished? Some professionals slant their stories for a specific market. Some just write the best story they know how and try it on all markets. A list of markets can be found in the writers' magazines. If you have a story you have faith in, you can start at the top and work down. Just keep two things in mind. If your story doesn't sell to the big national ones, but does sell to a minor market, be thankful. At the start be glad to publish anywhere. It's a terrific boost to the morale. Second, send your story to an *appropriate* market.

Long ago when I was working as an editor, there was a young authoress who sent us in a love story regularly every week. She apparently was working from a list of publishers and hadn't taken the trouble to study our requirements. If she had, she would have learned that we published men's magazines only.

Don't antagonize the editors. Some beginners are forever suspicious that their scripts are not being read, and they use every kind of device to check on the editor.

They'll transpose pages, turn pages upside down, lightly paste pages together. If the script comes back to them as it was sent out, they then dash off an angry letter to the editor, denouncing him. Don't be like that—unless you want to deliberately brand yourself a rank amateur.

Don't write an editor a letter introducing yourself or your script. He doesn't care who you are or what you are, or that the story is based on an incident in your Aunt Susie's life. All he's interested in is reading your story. Don't delay him. Let him get to it.

So there you are. Study and write. Persevere. Acquire a professional approach to your writing.

2

SEVEN POINTS FOR STORY BEGINNINGS

I DID NOT WRITE a salable first page until I came to realize that I was not a good enough writer to hold anyone by the sheer beauty and power of my writing. I "came to realize" the hard way, via a scrawled and exasperated note on a rejection slip: "Why did you wait to start your story on page ten?"

Was I angry? No. Bruised, but grateful, I bought some books on how to write and they told me to introduce my characters, set my scene, state my problem in the first page or two. In fact, they said I should get as much as possible into the first page.

First things first

I floundered around for the next couple of years trying to do as I'd been told—without success. But about this time I met a professional writer. Instead of telling me how to write openings, he took some of his own stories and showed me paragraph by paragraph the how and why of them. In three months I learned more than in the three previous years. And I began to sell my stories, too.

I would like to use a similar approach here, with some first pages from my own published stories, and show how they were done. But first, what goes into a first page:

1. a narrative hook (something like, "The sense of danger came to him like a half-remembered face; a nameless thing that hid in the steady throb of the packet's engines and gnawed at the security confidence had bred within him.")

2. *some setting* (so we can begin to picture the scene)

3. *the introduction of all main characters* (by name, if not on the scene)

4. *some characterization of the protagonist* (so that he begins to come alive)

5. *establishment of the emotional tone*

6. *start of the conflict*

7. *a hint at the problem*

Sometimes it is neither feasible nor possible to cram all these elements into the first page of a story, but I try to get in as many as possible.

Now here's the first manuscript page of a story. It is about a little boy whom nobody wants. He lives in a Home, and the story opens with a man and wife coming to find a child for adoption and the boy's craving to be the one chosen. That's his problem, to be wanted, and to have a father and mother. Sometimes a first page comes out without effort; more often it requires days of work; this one took three days to write. The lead:

When the man and the woman stepped into the room David held his breath. The woman was pretty and smiling, the man big and pleasant-faced. David had known they would be. From the upstairs window in the dormitory he had seen them get out of their car and come into the Home. Now the longing in him swelled and grew until it was nearly suffocating him.

In the first sentence I have introduced the man and the woman and David. And I have David holding his breath in order to give importance to their entrance into the room, as well as to plant a "Why did he hold his breath?" question in the reader's mind. In the second sentence I describe the couple briefly, and I purposely make them nice, the kind of people that David would surely want for a father and a mother, the kind that will make his disappointment all the more bitter when they turn him down for another child. The importance to him of this moment is made clear in the next two sentences, and here also I start setting my scene, with the words "dormitory" and "Home". In the last sentence I add to the "why", hoping to pull the reader on to the next paragraph:

Please, God, let me be the one, he prayed silently.

In the body of the story this boy, in his bitterness, rejects God; therefore, it is necessary to establish the religious tone of the story immediately. What better way than to have him pray? "Let me be the one," is his problem, *but only hinted at*. If the whole problem were stated in black and white so early, reader interest might be lost.

He stood by the window, a tall, thin, awkward boy, and waited while they looked around the big recreation room.

There were the other children busy at their work tables and blackboards and games, sixteen boys and girls between the ages of two and five.

In the first sentence of this paragraph David is described and the setting is added to. Note the use of the word "awkward," which helps explain why he has not been chosen before this. The second sentence is setting, and the ages of the other children are established.

David's fingers tightened on the model airplane in his hand. He held it a little higher, in front of his chest, where they would be sure to see it. It was his best, just finished. He'd put wax on it to make it shine. He'd put water on his hair, too, and combed it. He'd polished his shoes with a cloth.

I use the model airplane to show the difference in age between David and the other children. I show his pride in it, his wish to let this man and woman know that he can make and do things the other kids can't. I have him slick up his hair and polish his shoes to show his awareness (probably unconscious) of his shortcomings. I try to make David sympathetic.

Please, God.

He prays again. The religious tone of the story is hit at every opportunity.

They had to like him. For five years he had been in the Home; while other children, hundreds of them, had come and gone. He couldn't bear it if they didn't. He couldn't bear it another time.

This paragraph states his problem—subjectively and emotionally. We feel the upheaval in him. This is important because his reaction, when he is not chosen, is pretty violent. If his feelings at the start were not desperate, his reaction would seem without justification.

That's the first page of the story. There is hardly a word that is not there without a purpose. In fact, there is hardly a word in the entire story that does not have its purpose. The one thing I couldn't do in this first page was introduce the other main characters, the little boy who *is* chosen, and the Mother Superior; but they are both in there pitching on the second page.

Stories start on page one

Here's another story. The protagonist does not like cold weather, and he has come to sunny Florida to get warm and to work—though in an easy-going sort of way. This doesn't suit his fiancée, who is a fancy gal with ambitions for him. It does suit the "real" girl, whose father has sold him a popcorn and cold drink wagon and stayed on to show him how to run it. There's your triangle formula. Here's the conflict: the fancy fiancée wants the lad to go back to New York to a conventional job in her father's bank; he wants to stay with his popcorn wagon. He also starts to fall in love with the "real" girl.

It took a week or two of preliminary, spare-time thinking to organize the story in my mind and a day of hard, full-time thinking to decide how to start that first page. Inasmuch as the popcorn wagon represented the conflict, I wanted to establish it as quickly as possible. I decided to show it to the reader in the first paragraph, in the first line, no less:

> The trailer was a big, four-wheeled job painted red and silver, open on both sides and emblazoned with signs ad-

vertising the sale of Peanuts, Popcorn, Kandy-Krisp, Cold Drinks. Bill's feet were on one counter, his elbows on the other, and in between his long frame was precariously sustained by an up-ended orange crate.

The first sentence gives a picture of the trailer and more or less sets the mood of the story—at least, we feel it's not going to be anything very heavy. The second sentence introduces and starts to characterize the protagonist. By having him with his feet on the counter, I show his yen for the unconventional life and start the contrast between him and his fiancée, who is introduced in the next paragraph:

He was watching a girl coming toward him up the beach. Her high-heeled shoes were giving her a hard time in the soft sand and her green silk dress looked as out of place here as a bathing suit would on Fifth Avenue; but she was the most beautiful girl in all Florida, without any doubt. Her black hair was coiled around her head, and her figure was long and willowy, the kind that would make a Miss America look like a sea horse.

The "beach", the "sand", and "Florida" tell us where this is taking place. We get a picture of the fancy fiancée and find out the protagonist's feelings for her: ". . . she was the most beautiful girl in all of Florida, without any doubt." Get that "most beautiful." He thinks he is in love with her, but actually he is dazzled by her. This is one of many plants to establish that fact. The reader won't catch this one, but as the others come out the fact gradually will register.

One other point in that paragraph may be worth mentioning. I describe the girl's figure as "the kind that would make a Miss America look like a sea horse."

I could have said "like a tank" or "wash tub"; but I wanted to tie my similes in with the setting.

> She was as pale as a tourist, though; and her pallor was an uneasy reminder to Bill of the way she and her mother had flown down from New York the same day they'd received his wire. They were like a pair of jets out on a mission—with him as their target.

This paragraph starts the story moving. We don't yet know what the wire was about, but before the end of the page we do. Note that the mother is with the girl. The odds are two to one; later the father has his say via long-distance telephone, and then it's three to one. The phrase, "with him as their target," is the start of the conflict.

> She was nearly past the trailer when she spotted him. She stopped short, and Bill wondered how so much beauty could look so frozen all at once. When she walked slowly toward him he brought his feet down off the counter and stood up. Bill was in shorts and a striped jersey and his tan was the burned red of a week-old Floridian. He had blue eyes and a peeling nose, and his mouth was wide— and smiling usually.

The first two sentences are the girl's reaction to the trailer. Bill is described (straight narrative, to save time) and I feed in the information that he has been in Florida only a week. The last three words "and smiling usually" tell us that he knows he is about to get it in the neck. Why?

> She stopped a few feet away and her shocked gaze travelled over the trailer.
> "Don't tell me this is it?"

The trailer is "why." He has wired her that he bought a business instead of accepting a job in her father's bank. He has asked her to become the wife of a "budding peanut and popcorn tycoon." He ends up, of course, owning all the concessions on the beach and making twice as much as he would in the bank job.

In this story, as in the other, I don't introduce all the main characters on my first page; it wasn't possible or feasible. But here's a third story in which they are *all* introduced on page one, either by name or in the flesh. It's about a boy whose dog has been lost for three or four months. The dog has been returned to his home and the boy, but he doesn't seem to care for the boy any more and, to cap it off, the man who had found and kept him for those months wants to buy him. The kid is hurt. This has come at a time, too, when his mother has died and his father has married again. In giving up his dog, the boy begins to understand how his father could turn to another woman.

Because this story was to run only 3000 words, I had to open it as close to the climax as possible; I had to get into it fast. The best way to do this is by dialogue. The minute you start your characters talking they come alive. With dialogue, too, you can state your problem, give out information, build conflict. The percentage of dialogue in this story is very high. The first page:

"There was a long-distance telephone call for you while you were out, David," his stepmother said. "It was Tom Fenton."

He had paused at the head of the flight of steps leading down into the basement; now he turned back into the kitchen, staring at his stepmother in disbelief. "Where is he?" he whispered.

"In New York." Frances Gordeon wiped her hands on the red apron around her waist. She'd been baking when he'd come in and the kitchen was warm with the rich sweet odor of pastry. "That is, he *was* in New York. He's on the train now. He said he was taking the 2:10." She glanced at the clock on the wall. "It's three-twenty. He ought to be here in a few minutes."

David looked down at the package he was holding and was conscious of its coolness against the damp palm of his hand. He'd brought back a pound of meat, something special for Jeff, something to get the big Airedale to forget his broken leg and eat.

"Why didn't you tell him it's no use his coming here." David's voice rose sharply. "I don't want his two hundred dollars. I wouldn't take two thousand. Jeff's mine and he can't have him. Why didn't you tell him that?"

In this first page the scene has been set; the characters have been introduced; their characterization has been started; the emotional tone has been set; the conflict has emerged; and the problem has been more than just hinted at. What about one of the seven points—a narrative hook? The whole first page is our narrative hook. We want to know now, "What's going to happen when Tom Fenton arrives and David refuses to give up his dog?"

No two writers work exactly alike. Some race through the first draft and rewrite afterwards; others rewrite as they go along. I'm a middle-of-the-roader. But one thing I cannot do is start page two until page one reads, sounds, and feels right.

Getting these seven points—or even five or six of them—into your first page may seem a big job. It is; so work at it. Practice leads and first pages not just now and then, but every day. You will acquire confidence and know-how. And when you *know how,* you won't have to worry so hard over first pages. The seven points will be there; you will get them in subconsciously.

3

HOW TO PUT EMOTION INTO YOUR STORY

HAVE YOU EVER ASKED YOURSELF, "What is my purpose in writing a piece of fiction? What am I trying to do?" You are, of course, trying to write an interesting story, with good characterizations, with good dialogue, with good setting, and so on down the whole list of points of technique that go into putting together a first-class story. You naturally are trying to sell your story. You are trying, too, to satisfy an urge within yourself.

But what more specific purposes are you trying to accomplish? Are you trying to please the reader? Yes. Are you trying to make him feel something? Yes. Are you trying to make him feel emotion? Very definitely, yes.

The chief purpose of fiction is to arouse emotions within the reader. From the first to the last page that is your whole reason for writing. Whereas the article writer appeals to the intellect, the fiction writer appeals to the emotions. He tries every trick in the book to arouse these emotions to the highest pitch. Without emotion a story is a flat and dull and uninteresting thing. This cannot be stressed too strongly. Good emotion in a story is the sum-total of the proper use of all the other points of technique.

What are emotions? Intense emotions are love, hate, grief, anger, despair, fear, etc. They are basic and fundamental to life itself. They *are* life, and nearly everyone has experienced one or all at some time or another. Less intense emotions are feelings of suspense, sadness, contentment, admiration, pleasure, etc. Less intense emotions stir mild feelings within the reader. Intense emotions arouse stronger feelings within him. If the reader's emotions are aroused sufficiently, he will live the story with the characters. If a writer can do that, he has a sure sale for his story. He has fulfilled his job as a writer.

The direct approach to readers' emotions

All emotion falls into two categories. One is the emotion aroused directly within the reader. The other is the emotion aroused within the character and therefore indirectly within the reader. Let's take the first, arousing emotion directly within the reader, and give an example.

He was a tall, broad-shouldered young man with dark, uncombed hair, and eyes that were pleasant and blue— and wide-awake now as he listened to Lilly's cool voice from three thousand miles away.

"I've just come from a party at Panther Studios and had to call you before going to bed, darling. They've asked me to do another short for them. That means I won't be able to leave Hollywood for at least thirty days."

"Ouch," Bill murmured.

"We can be married six weeks from now as easily as one," Lilly said.

Bill's gaze was drawn to the picture of Lilly beside the telephone stand. Lilly of the blond hair and gorgeous figure, and the pouting, kissable lips. Beautiful, glamorous, fast-stepping Lilly. His Lilly for five whirlwind months.

"Don't be angry," Lilly said.

"I'm not," Bill groaned. "I just wish you'd told the studio you had more pressing business here in New York."

He suddenly remembered the wedding arrangements.

"They'll have to be postponed," Lilly said.

And there were the invitations. She'd asked half of New York.

"I'll give a statement to the papers changing the date."

There was a two-dollar pause, then she asked, "What've you done about the apartment? Have you cleaned out the mess?" [The mess referred to is a vegetable garden Bill is growing on his penthouse terrace.]

"Mess?"

"You know what I mean," Lilly said impatiently.

"I've started to," Bill hedged.

"You said by the time I got back you'd have everything out and it would be ready for the decorators."

Bill didn't answer.

"Don't put it off too long, my pet," and before he had a chance to reply, "Goodby, darling."

Bill looked at the receiver, then slowly put it back on the stand. He scowled at it. Maybe it was their conversation or maybe it was the early-morning hour, but there for an instant he'd had an unreasonable urge to tell Lilly to go sing a high C for herself.

In the opening of this scene (it is also the opening of

the story), a feeling of liking for Bill has been aroused within the reader. He is described as a big, broad-shouldered guy with *pleasant* blue eyes. A little further along, Lilly is described as a glamorous, fast-stepping girl with pouting lips—and a feeling of dislike is aroused within the reader. By simple descriptive *characterization,* then, two directly opposite emotions have been aroused directly within the reader.

How else were these emotions aroused? By *dialogue.* Bill is nice about the whole thing. Lilly is domineering, commanding, nasty. Even the words "my pet" were used deliberately to show her as being condescending.

Further along in the story, we meet the other girl, the real heroine. It is imperative that a feeling of liking for her is aroused in the reader. Here is how it is done. She is standing on the terrace of the penthouse below his.

> Her back was to him and all he could see of her was a pair of blue slippers, blue pajama legs, and a knee-length house coat and quite a lot of wavy brown hair. It was enough, though.
> When he coughed she turned and he saw that she was pretty.
> Her glance lifted to his window.
> "Have you seen Albert?" he inquired politely.
> She looked about her uncertainly.
> "Albert, or it could be Alberta," Bill explained, "is a cricket. He's escaped from his terrarium."
> Her voice was relieved. It was also soft and warm, and did funny things to Bill. "I'm afraid I haven't."
> "Poor Albert must have fallen down there?" He left it a question.
> The girl came forward hesitantly. She bent over, and her gaze scanned the concrete floor of the terrace.

"Albert," Bill informed the back of her head, "has always led a very sheltered life."

"It must be quite a problem these days to tell how much freedom one should give their crickets," the girl replied without looking up.

Bill chuckled. "I could come down and help you look for him."

"That's all right," she said. "I'm an old hand at hunting crickets. Besides, it won't be necessary now," she added and, sinking to her knees, made a grab at something on the cement. She wriggled forward and made another grab, then rose to her feet and held up her cupped hands triumphantly. "Albert. Or a reasonable facsimile thereof." Her eyes measured the distance to his window. "I guess you'll have to come down, after all, if you want to collect your livestock."

Six minutes later, in flannels and a blue sport shirt, Bill pressed the bell to apartment 14-C. The door opened almost immediately and Miss New Tenant stood before him. She had brushed her hair and touched color to her lips; and they were very nice lips, and she had very nice eyes, large and brown, and friendly.

Here Miss New Tenant is *characterized*. Her voice is soft and warm, and she has nice lips, and very nice eyes, large and brown, and friendly. We like her. We like her, too, because of her *dialogue*. It is gay and bantering, in sharp contrast to Lilly's imperious words.

In this scene we have done another thing. We have established a *mood* which continues throughout the body of the story. We have aroused a feeling in the reader of gaiety and light-heartedness. This is important since this is a light love story. Later on it looks as if Lilly is going to win Bill and make him get rid of his garden, and a feeling of suspense is created. At the end, Miss New Tenant wins him and we have a feeling of satisfaction.

We also arouse emotion through *action*. Here's an example:

Slade's foot drew back, then shot forward, kicking the puppy in the stomach with bone crunching force.

Indignation, anger, hatred, all are created in the reader directly. A grim mood is also established.

Another good way is through the use of sensory appeal.

Jim could hear Slade's heavy footsteps on the stairs, could smell his garlic breath even before he entered the room. Then the man himself lumbered through the doorway and stood glowering at him belligerently out of swollen, red-rimmed eyes.

Here we have created feelings of dislike and disgust. We have used the sensory appeals of sound, smell, sight. Only taste and touch are missing.

Emotional reactions

Now what about emotion aroused indirectly through the characters? The way to do this is through *reaction*. Let's go back to the cricket story a minute. At the end of the scene with Lilly, Bill reacts. He would like to tell Lilly to go sing a high C for herself. At this point we would like to, too, and so Bill's reaction sparks off a similar reaction in us, and our feeling of dislike is intensified. When Bill meets Miss New Tenant, he is struck by her looks, and her voice does funny things to him. He is beginning to react emotionally, and so is the reader.

Let's show now some more intense emotions aroused indirectly in the reader through a character's reactions. This is from another story:

> For the past minute she had been too shocked to say a word. To think, even. To do anything but sit and stare at him in dismay.
> *It can't be happening!*
> That was the first faint trickle of feeling beginning to penetrate the numbness around her brain.
> *It can't be! It can't! Not to us!*
> The trickle became a stream as everything inside of her erupted in violent rejection of what he had just told her.
> She wanted to laugh suddenly. Hysterically. That was what women did, didn't they, when their husbands—out of the clear blue—calmly announced the end of their marriage? They grew hysterical. Or weepy. Or some of them just died—down deep—quietly—
> She had been dead for more than a minute. That was the way it felt. The shock. The numbness. The collapse— the disintegration—of the whole world—her world.

Every word in this story opening is reaction; both physical and thinking. The girl is in emotional shock. Through her reactions the reader experiences the same emotions that she does, though to a lesser degree. This is more than just a story of divorce. It is a story of the threat to a man and a woman's love for each other. It is a universal experience. Not that every woman in the world is faced with divorce, by any means, or even contemplates it, but nearly all, at one time or another in their married life, perhaps in the depths of a quarrel, have felt that the end has come. To some this might bring relief, but to most it is a shattering thing. I wanted to write a story not of divorce, but of emotion, and I chose this subject deliberately because of its universality. The whole first scene of more than two thousand words is one emotion piled upon another.

Here's some more. This is emotion brought out in dialogue and conflict as well as by reactions. She has refused to give her husband a divorce, and he asks why:

> Jane drew a long full breath. There was hurt and indignation and anger—a determination—in her suddenly.
>
> "The answer should be perfectly obvious, Bill." She was still able to keep her voice as calm as his.
>
> He looked back at her blankly, waiting for her to explain.
>
> "What about the children?"
>
> He walked to a chair beside the fireplace and sat down. He sat on the edge and resting his elbows on his knees clasped his hands in front of him.
>
> "I know." Little lines appeared around his mouth and eyes and down each side of his face beside his nose. "Don't think I haven't thought of them."
>
> "How hard?" The anger and the indignation took an upward leap inside of her.
>
> "As hard as I've ever thought of anything, Jane."
>
> "Then how in heaven's name can you even consider a divorce?" It burst from her.
>
> He spread his hands out in front of him. "Kids adjust."
>
> "Never!" She said it with such positiveness she nearly shouted it. "That's an alibi, a conscience-saver, of the lowest and most cowardly sort."

Here the emotional strain is felt in both Jane and Bill. At the same time, the reader feels admiration for Jane because she is fighting to save her marriage. Suspense is also aroused. Will she succeed?

The next point to remember is to understate your emotion. Suppress it. The more you suppress an emotion, the stronger it becomes. The louder and brassier your emotion, the weaker it becomes. It becomes melodramatic, instead of dramatic, and your reader is more apt to laugh at your characters than to live the emotional experience with them.

How do you suppress emotion? Again by reactions. By understating. For example, Bill is engaged to one girl, but has just kissed another. I didn't write, "The fire of Nancy's kiss burned his lips; his heart pounded madly."

I wrote:

> The only comparison Bill could make with that moment was when he had been hit by a car years earlier. Only instead of a hospital bed he found himself standing afterward in the empty vestibule staring at the closed door of Apartment 14C. Nancy had drawn away, and they'd looked at each other in amazed silence. Bill hadn't apologized. Neither had she. She hadn't said a word.

Here's another example: I didn't write, "David burst into tears," but—"He stared at the little silver necklace dangling from his mother's neck. The light shone on it, wavy and sparkling, as though he were looking at it through a glass of water." That's reaction shown obliquely, or indirectly.

Then there's reaction by comparison and exaggeration. Joe's been kissed by his best girl, so we might compare him to a helicopter. We might write, "Joe had never felt like a helicopter before. He had never risen into the air before, straight up past the moon, higher and higher, until he knew he couldn't be more than a hundred miles or so from heaven. He had a feeling of lightheadedness and giddiness."

Or if she had slapped him we might say, "Joe had never been a mole before, trying to burrow down through Mrs. Miller's best Oriental rug and out of sight of the roomful of people staring at him." Both of these examples would be suitable for a light love story. They are more colorful than if I had merely said, "Joe was exhilarated," or "Joe felt like crawling away."

Now let's take a longer example of reactions under-written. Let's go back to the story of the orphan boy discussed in the previous chapter, "The Seven Points for Story Beginnings." David, you'll remember, wants to be adopted, but no one seems to want *him*. The day of the story he has been given the go-by once more for another boy. Here the Mother Superior tries to comfort him. She says:

> "God will hear your prayers."
> David shook his head fiercely.
> "Yes, he will." The Mother Superior's face was whiter, sterner than ever before.
> "He hasn't yet."
> The Mother Superior pressed her palms flat on the table.
> "If you love God—"
> "I don't," David gasped.
> "Yes, you do."
> "I don't." All the bitterness and resentment and disappointment of five years rushed to the surface before he could stop it. "I hate Him!"
> There was fresh shock, then hurt, in the Mother Superior's eyes. "You don't mean that." It was almost a whisper.
> "I hate Him." David repeated the words hoarsely.
> The Mother Superior sank back in her chair and stared at him. He could hear her expel the breath from her lungs in a deep sigh, and her face looked drawn and tired suddenly, as though she had run a long race only to come out the loser.

In this example, we have both characters reacting to each other in almost every line, David subjectively, the Mother Superior objectively. It is dramatic. *And it is understated.*

Then here's a scene between David and Billy a little bit later. David has just finished wishing Billy were dead. To keep this scene from becoming melodramatic I used the simplest words and reactions I could:

> Billy looked up at him. There were tears all over his cheeks. "I want my mother."
>
> David shut his eyes.
>
> "I want my mother."
>
> David was shaking so hard he could barely stand. "You'll have a mother in a couple of weeks," he said savagely.
>
> Billy stopped crying.
>
> "The lady who was here today." David fought down the jealousy and the envy that came with just talking about it. "Mr. Brown is going to be your father."
>
> David opened his eyes. Billy was crawling out from under the covers. He sat on the bed, looking up at him.
>
> "Will they be like my real father and mother?"
>
> David hesitated. Billy's real father and mother had died in a fire six months ago—he'd overheard two of the sisters talking about it. "Yes," he said.
>
> "Will I live with them?"
>
> "Yes."
>
> "Will they love me?"
>
> David tried to swallow the baseball in his throat. "Yes."

Writing emotion is not easy to do, but the technique can be mastered with constant practice and an awareness of what you are trying to do. But it *has* to be in your story from the first to the last page. Your whole reason for writing, remember, is to arouse emotions within your reader.

🖎 4

WHAT IS A SCENE?

BEFORE BEGINNING ANY DISCUSSION OF SCENE, the difference between scene and scenery should be made perfectly clear. Many writers think of them as one and the same thing. I did myself for a number of years. But eventually I discovered that scenery is setting, and scene a unit of plot.

Let's take a stage play. The curtain goes up and we see a living-room. We see a table in the center, a sofa against the wall, an easy chair on either side of the fireplace, a picture over the mantel, the inevitable TV set. This is scenery, or setting. On the stage we see it; in a fiction story it has to be shown to the reader with words.

Scene, as we have said, is a unit of plot. It is the action that takes place within a setting. A short story, or a novel, is made up of a series of scenes leading to a climax. A class of mine once analyzed five hundred short stories to find out the answers to some questions that were disturbing them. One of the questions answered was what was the average number of scenes found in these short stories. They ranged from one all the way up to ten or more, but the average was from three to four. One scene is sparse; ten scenes are confusing; three or four usually will do the job and make for simplicity, and therefore strength.

Component parts for a scene

But what *is* scene? What are its components? The first thing I think of when I am planning a scene is conflict. Every scene must have conflict, just as the whole story must have it. It is the one indispensable ingredient of a story. There have been some excellent stories written with only one character ever appearing. The conflict could be man against nature (storm, flood, etc.) and/or man against himself (a character weakness such as fear), but in these cases, the nature conflict, or the man-against-himself conflict, assumes the proportions of a living character and becomes the opposing force.

The formula for a scene is as old as fiction itself. Let's take a story with two characters in conflict. The first thing to do is have the characters meet, head-on. Suppose a character, David, learns that his older brother is going to trap his pond. We bring the two main characters together, in action and dialogue. They Collide. Now what is the Reason for this Collision? David doesn't want his pond trapped; his brother does. What comes after that? The Conflict over the trapping, David's opposition and his attempts to stop it. The Outcome of the Conflict follows. David fails in his attempts.

These are four components of a scene, but there is a fifth. Do you remember learning in school that in writing a theme or thesis, the final sentence of one paragraph should be a lead into the next paragraph? The same applies to scenes in fiction, only I think "lead" is too pale a word. "Hook" is better. You hook your reader into the next scene. You grab him by the neck and yank him over into it. You make your hook so strong and intriguing and so full of suspense that the reader *has* to go on reading to find out what happens. The reader *has* to find out whether or not David is going to be able to stop his brother from trapping his pond.

So we have the five components of a scene:

> Collision
> Reason for the collision
> Conflict
> Outcome
> Hook

Three or four scenes are best for a short story, but in a novel they can run up into the hundreds in number. This does not, however, include transition scenes. A transition scene is a short scene of a few paragraphs bridging two scenes. It is possible, and very often advisable, simply to cut from one scene to the next. Other times a bridge is necessary for a smooth effect. This transition scene does not have the five components of a full scene. It is usually used to cover a transition of time, or space, or both.

For example, if one scene ends in a bus station, and you want to begin the next two hours later in the protagonist's office, instead of cutting abruptly with something like, "Two hours later Bill walked into his office, etc.," you could write, "Bill glanced at his watch and saw that he had two hours to kill before his office opened. He walked down the rain-swept street to the all-night restaurant on the corner and ordered a cup of coffee. When the counter man brought it he scowled down into his cup without touching it. Even though he and Mary had argued all the way from Boston, and she had flatly turned down his proposal after making it very plain that she never wanted to see him again, he knew he would see her again, and no later than that night. He wasn't afraid of her father the way she was. Or was he? Mr. Horton was a huge man with a violent temper, and not above resorting to physical violence."

If we were to have Bill simply walk down the street, drink a cup of coffee, and then go to his office, it would be pure action and pretty boring. In this transition, we have added his thoughts about the girl and her father. Instead of bringing the story to a stop, we have advanced it. When Bill decides to see Mary again the reader is eager to see what happens.

Changing scenes

Now we come to one of the fine points of scening. When does a scene end? When the setting changes? It can. But the chief purpose of a scene, as with a complete story, is to arouse emotion within the reader. The end of a scene comes when there is a break in the dominant emotion of your scene, when a crisis has been reached and the emotion turns down. This can be accomplished within the space of one setting. Or it may require several changes of setting. These changes of setting may give the appearance of changes in scene, but until the emotional crisis has been reached, they are not. Let's take an example: A husband and wife are on a train speeding towards New York. They are in conflict over something. She could be a career woman, and her career is interfering with their marriage. She could be earning more money than he is, and he resents it. They are still in conflict when the train reaches the city. They take a cab to a hotel. The conflict continues throughout the ride. They reach their hotel and go up to their room. The conflict is still between them. But at a point of crisis, when the author has played the conflict and the emotion to the limit, the husband says he has had it, and leaves. That is the end of your scene.

Going down in the elevator the husband may be determined never to see his wife again. Or he may have regrets. He may feel sadness at the turn of events. This brief scene would be your transition scene. The next main scene could begin in the lobby. He might meet an old flame. He might turn to her for solace. This would begin the build-up of another dominant emotion, in him and, therefore, in the reader. This, too, would lead to a crisis, and another change in, or intensification of, emotion.

A thorough understanding of this point of technique simplifies the writing of your story. It makes for unity in your story, rather than confusion. It sharpens your crises, and assures a rising and falling action. Few stories can start on a point of crisis (which they should) and move straight uphill for five thousand words to the climax. The breaks in conflict and emotion are necessary for relief. The reader would otherwise grow exhausted before the climax was ever reached.

Learning story technique is a little like looking at a statue. You have to look at a statue from all angles before you see it as a whole. Let's look at scenes from a new angle. I have divided this "new look" into four categories: 1) The scenes leading to the climax of my story will have: 2) My opening scene will have: 3) My middle scene(s) will have: 4) My last scene will have:

Here they are with a few brief notes:

THE SCENES LEADING TO THE CLIMAX OF MY STORY WILL HAVE:

1. A setting—some indication of the time and place.

Is the action taking place in daytime or nighttime, in spring or in fall, in this century or the last? This should be established as close to the beginning of a scene as possible. As well as identifying himself with the protagonist, or lead character, a reader likes to identify himself with the setting. Nothing is more destructive to this identification than to have him think that the story is set in the present and that he is in a hotel bedroom, only to discover, after the action has gone on for some time, that he is in a medieval dungeon. The setting should be established immediately at the opening. You can do this with possibly one word, "living-room," or "railroad station," then later in the scene describe the living-room or the railroad station more fully.

2. A collision of the characters

This collision should take place as near the opening of your scene as possible. Don't preface it with useless action, or lengthy passages of description. Don't have your protagonist leave home, stop for a newspaper, drink a cup of coffee, take a bus to his office, and then start a fight with his boss. At the opening have him fighting with his boss. Or don't spend a page describing the office before the collision starts.

3. Conflict

This is the body of your scene. Always remember—make it strong.

4. Crises of their own—apart from the major crisis.

By major crisis we mean the climax of your story. In a four-scene story the major climax would be at the end of the third scene. The two preceding scenes would each have their own, lesser, crises.

5. An outcome—a definite win, lose, or draw, but *not* a dead-end halt

6. A hook

7. A dominant emotion

This should not be confused with the major emotional tone of the whole story. In a light love story the major emotional tone would be gay and light-hearted. At the same time, the dominant emotion of the various scenes could be of a more serious nature. Love is basically serious. If it is in doubt whether or not the protagonist will win the girl a feeling of suspense is aroused. If he temporarily does lose the girl the reader despairs with him.

MY OPENING SCENE WILL HAVE:

1. The "seven points" for the first page
   (This is covered in Chapter 2.)
2. A development of the seven points
   Fuller characterization, setting, etc.
3. The beginning of the story lines
   a. Character line
   b. Action line
   (This is covered in the final chapter.)

4. Any necessary plants and foreshadowing

The best way to explain a plant is to give an illustration. This is a classic one. A dear, sweet old lady shoots the villain at the climax of the story. It would be wholly unbelievable if she were suddenly to whip a gun out of her knitting bag. Early in the story, therefore, the gun must be shown to the reader. Let the reader see her putting it in her knitting bag. Then it doesn't come as such a surprise. Thus the gun is *planted*.

Foreshadowing is a promise to the reader of conflict or danger to come. For example, "When Bill looked into Drago's piercing, hate-filled eyes, he knew the man was spoiling for a fight." (The fight might not occur for three or four thousand words.) This gives a story suspense and interest.

5. An especially effective hook

When an editor reads a manuscript, he can usually tell by the end of the first page whether or not it has merit. If it has, he'll go on reading through the first scene. If the body of the scene is good, he'll read to the end of it. Now comes the crucial moment. If there is no hook, or the hook is weak, the editor's interest may lag and he may put your script aside. That's why the hook at the end of the first scene should be especially effective. Hook your editor into scene two, and you're almost assured of a complete reading.

MY MIDDLE SCENE (S) WILL HAVE:

1. The protagonist working at his problem. The story problem should be fully stated in the first scene. Now, in the middle scenes, the protagonist must

solve his problem. He tries, and fails. He tries again, and fails again. Only at the climax does he win.

2. Most of the obstacles that hinder him

When he fails to solve his problem it is because he has run into obstacles that snow him under temporarily.

3. The main character's motivations

To be real, characters must be motivated. There must be reason for their actions. This motivation, especially of the protagonist, must be brought out either in the first scene, or no later than the beginning of the second. Without proper motivation your characters never live.

4. A fuller development of these elements established in the opening

      a. Characterization
      b. Conflict
      c. Plants and foreshadowing

5. The story climax

    (Discussed in the chapter on Plot.)

MY LAST SCENE WILL HAVE:

1. Brevity without loss of pace

Your last scene should be short, but should not be rushed. If the pace has been at a trot for four thousand words, don't gallop through the last five hundred. It is a strong temptation to chop off a story and get it into the mails. Resist the temptation.

2. Evidence of definite character growth

Fast action adventure stories are often lacking in this growth of character. They rely solely on the action for effect. But if you are writing a character story, your protagonist is not the same person at the end of the story that he was at the beginning. He has changed, usually for the better. If he has been struggling with a character flaw, have him "come to realize" it at the end, thereby overcoming it.

3. Any loose ends tied up

Supposing you have a triangle love story. At the climax, with all three characters on scene, the girl chooses the protagonist. "Oke," the protagonist says. "Let's go get the license," and so ends the story. That won't do. What about the other guy? What happens to him? Does he just evaporate into thin air? If he's the villain type, at least give the reader the satisfaction of seeing him defeated. Suppose he's the lady-killer type, but not too bad a guy. Throw him a reward, such as another girl, and so keep him in character. Whatever you start you must finish. If you give a secondary character a problem of his own to resolve, you must resolve it. Don't leave it dangling.

4. An emotional lift for the reader

This is done at the very end of the story, in the last few lines, in action, or in dialogue, or in reaction. Its purpose is to give the reader a feeling of pleasure, or gratification, at the outcome of the story.

When planning a story, think it out in terms of scenes. By the time you are ready to write, you will then have a clear image in your mind of each scene. Don't start your story until these images are clear, the scenes complete. When they are, the story will start writing itself in your head. Then it is simply a matter of putting it down on paper.

~≈≈ 5

HOW IMPORTANT IS CONFLICT?

SOME WRITERS and critics believe characterization to be the most important element of fiction technique. Others believe conflict to be the most important. I belong to the second group. Long ago I learned how to create characters who were not in conflict. They were, of course, merely sketches of characters. Then I discovered that I could not write strong conflict without also creating character and, immediately, instead of writing *sketches* I began writing *stories*. I discovered that if I wrote conflict, and gave that conflict *direction*, it was almost impossible not to have a story.

Conflict brings out character in a person, whether he be live or fictional. Suppose we write about a man getting up in the morning and starting out his day's activities. He shaves, brushes his teeth, eats his breakfast, reads the morning paper. We detail his actions, and thoroughly describe him. What do we have? Absolutely nothing. Nothing, that is, in the way of a story. But suppose we give this same man an affliction; let's say he's partially paralyzed and he rebels against his affliction. He stumbles, falls, drops things, and each time he does, he wants to lie down and give up. He doesn't, though. He grits his teeth and tries again.

Now we have a real character, and an interesting one. Why? This man is fighting the battle of his life. The reader feels sympathy for him and wants him to beat his affliction. The reader feels disappointed when he lies down but cheers the man when he gets up and tries again. Strong emotions are aroused in the reader. If the outcome of the battle is in doubt—which it should be at times—suspense is built. Will he win or lose his battle? Now we have the beginnings of a *story*. But it still does not have enough substance to it.

What can we do to give it more substance, more depth? We can give our man another conflict. Suppose he has a wife who loves him very much and wants to help him. But she knows that the worst thing she can do is sympathize with him and coddle him. He will almost surely turn to her for strength, become dependent on her, give up the struggle.

It almost kills her to have to do it, but she holds aloof. When he shows signs of giving up, she taunts him and calls him a quitter. He is hurt and angry, he grows bitter. At times he even hates her. But her attitude strengthens his backbone, and, instead of quitting, he fights even harder.

To heighten the suspense, his anger against his wife might reach such serious proportions that their marriage starts to break up. He might even go so far as to leave home, or tell her to leave.

Conflicts in fiction—and life

This double conflict, which gives our story substance and depth, comprises two of the three conflicts in fiction —or in life, for that matter. The three conflicts are well known. They are:

1. Man against man (or woman, or a group of either, or both)
2. Man against himself
3. Man against nature

Let's discuss these three conflicts. The first one, man against man: Most straight action stories are built on this conflict. The protagonist wants something and is kept from it by someone. Or he has something that someone wants and will not give it up. In the case of the paralyzed man, the protagonist wants his wife's sympathy and help. When she doesn't give it to him, he is thrown into conflict with her.

Man-against-man conflict can be between two individuals; or it can be between an individual and a group of opponents. The protagonist could be an honest politician fighting against the corruption and dishonesty of a political machine. He could be fighting the machine as a whole, and/or its members individually, from its top man down to its muscle men. He could be fighting the top man legally or at the polls; he could be fighting the machine's muscle men physically, when they try to rough him up and intimidate him.

In another story your protagonist could be defending himself against a town of several thousand angry citizens. Suspected of thievery, he could fight his accusers by defending himself in court, or he could fight them by trying to prove that one of them is the real thief. This is man-against-man, although thousands of opponents are involved. If the fight is in court, the protagonist's opponent might be the prosecutor. If the fight is to find the real thief, his opponent might be one principal accuser. The prosecutor and the one accuser represent the town or group. Having one opponent represent the group spotlights the struggle and gives simplicity and, therefore, strength, to the story line.

As another example of man against a group, you might have a protagonist who has to overcome the opposition of his best girl's family before he can marry her. He must win over father, mother, brothers, sisters, aunts, uncles, perhaps even the family dog which bites him every time he comes to call on his girl.

Where man against man is conflict turned outward against flesh-and-blood opponents, man against himself is conflict turned inward against his own self. This conflict is one of character. The struggle is usually between strength and weakness within a character, between good and bad forces trying to gain control over his actions. A man has a dangerous duty to perform, and he is afraid. His man-against-himself conflict is his struggle to overcome his fear. Another man has stolen some money, and his inner conflict is whether to return the money or keep it. Each is fighting a weakness within his character, a bad force, which, if he were the protagonist of a story, would dominate him all the way up to the climax of the story. The greater his weakness, the more suspense there will be. The greater his struggle against this weakness, the more interesting, and the better rounded, will be his character.

The third conflict is man against nature. Nature can be a flood, drought, hurricane, blizzard, earthquake, famine, pestilence, etc. Stories have occasionally been written with one of these elements as the sole conflict. Like straight man-against-man stories, they lack substance. It is difficult to hold a reader's interest in a protagonist who, for five thousand words, simply wades through deeper and deeper snow drifts. Man-against-nature conflict is used mostly in combination with man against himself and/or man against man.

Let's go back to our paralyzed man for a minute and see if we can add a nature conflict to his other conflicts. Suppose he and his wife live on a boat. Suppose a hurricane is blowing up, and their boat is anchored in an open, exposed piece of water. He has to move it to a safer berth. Fighting against wind and rain and rough water, he finally gets the anchor up, starts the engine, steers the boat inshore, anchors again, or, better and more difficult still, he ties up to some trees. His wife doesn't lift a hand to help him, and his bitterness and resentment reach a climax in this scene. At the end, after he has finished and is lying on the deck exhausted, his wife gently points out that he has done a job that would ordinarily require two able-bodied men. Desperation and anger gave him superhuman strength, but he isn't so blind he can't see, she says, that though he may be partially paralyzed, he's as good as any man, certainly in spirit. He sees, and his battle against all three conflicts is won.

Moving a story forward

It isn't always possible, or feasible, to put all three conflicts in a story. The two most commonly used in combination are man against man and man against himself. I never write a story that doesn't include man against himself. As we have said, it gives depth and substance to a story, and characters in conflict are what an editor is looking for. This conflict is best brought out in dialogue and thoughts, which are the action that gives a story forward movement, a must in all fiction writing.

Now let's take a couple of published stories and see how these conflicts were used. The idea for the first story came orginally from a newspaper clipping, one of the best sources for story material. It told of a boy whose dog became stuck in a culvert. All efforts to free the dog failed, and neighbors decided the only way to get him out was to dig him out. But the culvert extended under a man's front yard, and the man, out of pure meanness, refused to let anyone dig up his yard. The problem stuck in my mind for almost two years before I did anything about it. It stuck because it offered a problem loaded with conflict.

Then one day I sat down to think the story out. I thought first of making this the boy's story, but that seemed pretty trite. Neither did it give me much opportunity to include a man (boy) against man conflict. I decided to use the man as my protagonist. Meanness was an unsympathetic and inexplainable motive for his refusing to let his yard be dug up, so the next thing I had to do was think up a better one, one that offered possibilities for character conflict. I thought for a week and finally came up with one that was not only sympathetic and understandable, but one that provided my man-against-himself conflict.

I made my protagonist a farmer who has been pauperized by several years of drought. He is not in active conflict with nature during the time lapse of the story, but nature in the form of the drought is there all the same, governing his actions and his fate. The only crop he has left is a small strawberry patch. Instead of using a culvert, which wouldn't be likely to extend under his strawberries, I used an abandoned well pipe. The boy's dog has fallen into this to a depth of eight or ten feet, and the only way to get him out is to dig down and cut the pipe off below him. But this would necessitate digging up the whole patch. The boy's father insists that this be done; the protagonist says no. Now we have our man-against-man conflict.

But this makes the protagonist an unsympathetic character, so the next step was to find a motivation, or reason, for his refusal. I decided to give him a son, a boy, who has suffered a fall and is crippled for life. The boy is in pain, and the money from the strawberry patch is to be used to buy a special bed to make the boy more comfortable. The protagonist's inner conflict is whether he should help the dog or his boy.

In this story all three conflicts were utilized—two directly, one indirectly. Here's a sample of the man-against-man conflict from this story:

"The next one to put a shovel in that dirt gets a load of buckshot in the legs," Dan warned.

"Well, I'll be damned," Wingate said in a flat, disbelieving voice.

Johnny moved close to his father. His eyes were despairing.

"This whole dried-up patch isn't worth what I paid for that pup." Wingate's arm swept a short, angry arc around him. "You mean to stand there and tell me you'd shoot a man for that?"

"I've told you four times," Dan reminded him. "Isn't that enough?"

The blood rose into Wingate's already red and sweating face. "I've met every kind of ornery character in my lifetime, but you, Clements—"

"Get off my land," Dan interrupted harshly.

Wingate glared at him, the anger and disbelief growing in his eyes. Then deliberately he turned his back and, picking up a shovel, began to dig.

Now let's take another story. Jane and Bill are desperately in love. But Bill has a wife, and Jane has a husband, and each couple has two young children. In order not to make them too unsympathetic, I have Bill's wife wedded to her club work, and Jane's husband wedded to his business; consequently, both marriages are on the rocks. Bill wants to marry Jane, but Jane is hesitant to divorce her husband because she doesn't want to hurt the children. Her conflict with her husband and her conflict with Bill when he presses her to marry him comprise her man-against-man conflict. Throughout the story, she is torn between her love for her children and her love for Bill. What should she do? She sways first one way, then the other. This inner struggle between what she thinks is right, and what she really wants, Bill, is her man-against-himself conflict. This conflict is the chief conflict in the story.

Here's a sample of how it was handled:

"Please say you'll be my wife," Bill pleaded.

A shiver ran through her. A fresh groan of anguish escaped her lips.

"Please say it, Jane."

She felt the last of her resistance melt away before his plea. "Yes," she heard herself gasp. "Yes, Bill. Yes. Yes. Yes."

Then later:

Jane had known it wasn't going to be easy to break up a home, wasn't going to be just a simple matter of telling Henry, and then the children, and then going off to Reno. But here she was—with nothing more than a suspicion that Sally [her daughter] knew—feeling the pangs of guilt and remorse already.

Suddenly she wasn't sure she could do it to Sally and Mike! Nor to Bill's children either! She would have to tell Bill tonight that she needed more time to think.

Then still later:

Jane started to speak. To tell Bill—

He stopped her. "I'm crazy in love with you, Jane."

Jane shut her eyes. And so was she, crazy in love with him. Crazy was the only word to describe the feeling. Crazy, meaning totally. Crazy, meaning hopelessly, helplessly.

His voice was determined. "The quicker this is done, the easier it will be on everyone."

She tried to deny that. She tried to tell him that they should wait. She tried to tell him all the things she had prepared in her mind.

But the words stuck somewhere in her throat. She couldn't say them. She felt robbed of her speech. It was as though she had been stricken dumb.

Man against man, man against himself, man against nature—at least two of these conflicts must be in your story. And they must be strong. If they're not, then make them strong; intensify them. Writing strong conflict may sound like a big order, but it isn't. As we have pointed out, many of the other elements of technique —character, suspense, emotion—spring from conflict. They emerge automatically, as a natural result of the conflict. And when that happens the whole business of story writing becomes far easier.

6

HOW TO CHARACTERIZE

GOOD CHARACTERIZATION is as indispensable to a story as strong conflict. It's been a long time since I've read Dickens' "A Christmas Carol," and I don't remember the story too well, but the character of Scrooge stands out vividly in my mind. It's been almost as long since I read *Gone With The Wind,* and the story actions are vague in my memory, but not so the characters of Rhett Butler and Scarlett O'Hara. It's the same with Hemingway's *The Old Man and The Sea:* The character of the old man stands out more vividly in my mind than the battle with the shark.

The action, settings, plots of these stories are essential in the development of a well-rounded story, but each in itself will not sustain a story. Good characterization will. You can be weak in many of the elements of technique, but you cannot be weak in characterization if you want to become a selling writer.

"Seeing" and "knowing" story characters

Characterization is achieved by two methods: 1. description of a character's appearance and actions—his physical appearance, and how he dresses, walks, talks, etc.; and 2. an analysis of the character himself—the sort of person he is, his traits, and how he thinks and feels. With the first we *see* the character. With the second we *know* the character. Neither one of these alone will present a vivid, well-rounded character to the reader. In combination, the two methods complement and aid each other. For example:

> A tall, gaunt man, Seth Adams shuffled down the street, his lined face twisted with worry, his thin shoulders hunched forward as though braced against the ills of the world.

In this sentence we *see* Seth Adams. He is tall and gaunt and thin and beaten down by some sort of trouble. We could go on to describe him more fully, put clothes on him, give the color of his eyes, etc. We would have the beginnings of a character, but we would not really *know* him. Let's see how *we* can get to *know* him:

> A tall, gaunt man, Seth Adams shuffled down the street, his lined face twisted with worry, his thin shoulders hunched forward as though braced against the ills of the world. If there were only some way to help his friend, Ben Lowe, he thought. If there were only something he could do. He would gladly give Ben the shirt off his back.

Now we know a lot about Seth Adams. We know he is kind, generous, unselfish, the sort of person to whom friendship means something. Suppose we change his thoughts to:

He should have known that Ben Lowe would ask him for money. What did Ben think he was, a bank? So what if Ben's wife was sick and needed a doctor? He could have asked someone else, couldn't he, instead of bothering him?

Here's a different Seth Adams, miserly, and selfish. In both instances we *know* him by his thoughts. Through his thoughts we have given him character traits, good in the first example, bad in the second.

How do we let the reader *see* a character? We can do it statically, by *description;* and dynamically, by *action.* Let's take static characterization first. We characterize statically by:

1. Name

Much about a character can be revealed by the use of an appropriate name. If your protagonist is young and pleasant and likable, give him a pleasant name like Bill Hulett or Johnny Adams, or Pete Baldwin. If he's the rugged type, make use of harsh consonants and call him Preston Britt. If he's an oily sort of character, tag him with a name like Benny Leach. Names for your characters should be chosen with great care and thought.

2. Age

I try to establish the ages of my characters as soon as possible, especially of my hero and heroine. You can't afford to let your reader think your protagonist is forty years old when he is actually a teen-ager, or vice versa. The readjustment to the correct age is distracting and will spoil any picture of your protagonist that you may be trying to build in the reader's mind

3. Bodily appearance

If you were walking down the street and suddenly came face to face with Abraham Lincoln, you would instantly know much of his character from his bodily appearance. You would see a tall, gaunt man, his shoulders bowed with the cares and burdens of a nation torn by strife. You would see a man saddened by the times, with compassion, love, faith, mirrored in every line of his craggy face, a simple man, but a man, withal, of extraordinary courage and strength.

Suppose, for contrast, you were suddenly to meet Teddy Roosevelt. Now you would see a stockily built, bulldog-faced man. You would see a man exuding strength and energy, a vibrant, self-assured man.

4. Clothing

One man wears wholesome tweeds, another wears flashy, checked suits and vests. Two entirely different characters are created in the reader's mind. Dress a woman up in diamonds and loud clothes. Is she the same person as a woman who wears conservative clothes and little or no jewelry?

5. Occupation

If a character's occupation can be given immediately at the opening of your story, you have gone a long way toward characterizing him. You present an immediate picture of the *type* of person he is. You also present the setting of your story. You say a character is a farmer, and a picture of a farmer and a farm springs to the reader's mind. It's very general, but it classifies the character. For contrast, let's say your character is a lawyer. The reader forms an instant picture of a well-educated, well-dressed, conservative type of man. Both characters are types, but naming their occupations starts the development of their characterizations. Later on you can breathe life into them by giving them traits that individualize them.

6. Surroundings

Let's put our lawyer in his study at home. Let's describe his study. There are shelves full of law books, but there is also a picture of his wife and two children on his desk, more pictures of them on the walls, a big portrait of his wife over the fireplace. By this simple static description we tell the reader that our lawyer is a family man, proud of his wife and children. Or, instead of pictures, let's cover the walls with trophies of fish. Hanging from pegs are half a dozen or more rods and reels. Now we know he is an outdoor man, a sportsman, as well as a lawyer.

7. Facial expression in repose

Meanness will show in a man's face, just as kindness will—or friendliness, hostility, moodiness, or cheerfulness. By describing a person's face in repose you reveal his character.

8. Posture

One man slouches in his chair—he is lazy, listless, possibly shiftless. Another man sits stiffly erect—he is alert, energetic, alive.

Let's turn now to dynamic characterization. We characterize dynamically, in action, by:

1. Gesture

I have a friend who is very unsure of himself. Whenever we engage in conversation, he jabs his finger in my chest anxiously to emphasize his words. I have another friend, a woman, who is so vain about her beautiful clothes she constantly draws attention to them by touching and fingering them. Her gestures reveal her character.

2. Walk

The way a person walks tells us much of his character. If a man walks with a bounce in his step, we know he is energetic, full of life. If he sidles, we know he is shifty. If he slouches, the chances are he is lazy and shiftless. Thus we can characterize with a single verb, slouched, sidled, bounced.

3. Tone of voice

A rude man speaks in a rude way. He speaks harshly, insolently, discourteously; he speaks with a sneer in his voice. A kindly man speaks in a kindly way. He is thoughtful of the feelings of others.

4. Dialogue

Not only does a rude man speak in a rude way, the words he utters are rude, coarse, vulgar. The words a kindly man uses are considerate, sympathetic, understanding.

5. Facial movement

We have mentioned Facial Expression in Repose. This should not be confused with Facial Movement. In repose a person's face might be calm and placid. In rage it might become contorted and suddenly reveal that person as having a violent and explosive nature.

Stimulus and response

We have briefly presented the various methods of revealing character, statically, by description, and dynamically, in action. Let's say that you have let us *see* your protagonist. You have given us a picture of him.

We know something about him. But still we don't really *know* him. We can get to know him, though, through his thoughts and by his reactions to given stimuli.

If five people were presented with the same stimulus, no two would be likely to react to it in the same way. If danger were the stimulus, one might faint, another run, another meet it with courage, another try to talk his way out of it. The character of each one would be different. If death of a loved one were the stimulus, the same five people again would react differently. One might refuse to admit it and withdraw from the world, another would meet it with faith, another with courage, another with despair. The way each of these characters reacts tells us the sort of person he is.

Why, you may be wondering, do five people react so completely differently to the one stimulus? The answer is that each one has different character traits which *are* his character. In short-short stories and in many short stories, the characters are usually flat; that is, they are one-dimensional; they usually have one dominant character trait. Characters in relief are those which have more than one character trait, most often one dominant trait and many minor traits. This type of character is found mostly in novels where there is plenty of space for development.

How do people acquire their character traits? Some acquire them through their environment. Still others have their traits moulded in them by some fateful and vitally dominant act or event in their lives. In a story a character's dominant trait governs, or directs, all his actions. But it is not enough just to give the character's trait; you must give a reason for it. You must give a *reason* for his *actions*. You must *motivate* your character.

For example: Let's say a man is woman-shy. This is his dominant character trait. But why is he woman-shy? Perhaps he saw this trait in his father and, small-boy-like, tried to be just like him. This is weak motivation and makes for an unsympathetic character. Suppose then that all through his formative years he was teased by girls because of an affliction, say, a terrible case of acne. This is stronger, and stirs our understanding. But suppose this man, quite recently, fell very deeply in love with a woman, and she jilted him in a cruel way. Now he has both our understanding and our sympathy. If he were woman-shy for no reason at all, your story would lack substance. It would be what the editors call "unconvincing."

I have my own way of characterizing my protagonist, both in my short stories and in my novels. It may not be the best way but it works for me. I describe my character statically as near the opening of my story as I can. I do not give a complete picture of him, because I do not want to stop my story. I give whatever is necessary for the reader to see him. I characterize him more fully later in the story, dynamically, through action. Here's an example of what I mean:

> Pete rolled over on his blanket and, propping up his head, looked up and down the beach. There was plenty of sun and blue sky and sand but it was a little too early in the morning for customers. Only a few cars were backed up against the dunes. The beach was almost deserted except for a long sand sailer, its triangle of canvas a brilliant red against the blue ocean, skimming up the beach toward him.
>
> He'd opened up for business half an hour ago. He'd set

up his camera, his portable chemical stand, his big striped umbrella, his sign advertising, "Your Picture Taken on Ferdinand for 25 Cents." Ferdinand, his live ox, saddled and bridled and with a big artificial rose pinned between his ears, stood near by, dozing in the sun and contentedly chewing his cud. Until they saw those jaws moving rhythmically many a tourist had thought him stuffed.

Pete lay back. His costume was a pair of faded shorts and, when he was working, a pith helmet. He was six feet, brown-haired, one hundred and seventy pounds and had a golden tan.

I have set the scene in the two opening paragraphs. I have done more than this. I have started to characterize Pete by his occupation. It's a pretty easy-going occupation and, therefore, he's a pretty easy-going guy. He is lying on a blanket, sunning himself as he waits for business. In the third paragraph I have started his physical characterization with thirty words of static description.

Now let's characterize the heroine. The sand sailer rams into his ox and upsets him. Pete finds a girl pinned underneath the sailer.

He looked down into the bluest pair of eyes. Above them was hair the color of sea oats. On her hands and knees she crawled out from under the sand sailer and stood beside him. She came about to his chin and was beautiful, even to *his* eyes. She was a creamy goddess in a blue bathing suit.

In this paragraph I have characterized the secondary character statically, *through Pete's eyes*. I, as the author, try always to keep strictly out of my stories. In characterizing Pete I have given the reader a glimpse of him.

Later in the story the reader gets to *know* him, through his thoughts, and through his reactions.

We have said that good characterization is indispensable to a story. Let's put that differently, to make it sound stronger. Let's say that without good characterization you won't have a salable story. Fortunately, however, it is one of the easiest points of technique to learn. It simply takes practice, and lots and lots of it. For years I wrote character exercises in my spare time, in trains and in buses, and in restaurants while waiting to be served. It takes only a piece of scratch paper and a pencil. Why not write twenty exercises a day? Why not start now?

7

HOW TO USE DIALOGUE

NO OTHER ELEMENT of technique performs as many functions as dialogue. It is the work horse of fiction. Occasionally you will find stories in which the dialogue is kept to a minimum, perhaps ten percent of the total wordage; but in most stories the percentage is much higher, running to fifty percent or more. Stories in which there is little or no dialogue make for slow, heavy reading. Dialogue gives them life. When you are writing dialogue, you are creating as in no other way, simply because dialogue *does* perform so many functions. What are these functions? Let's run through them briefly, then give some examples.

What dialogue does for a story

Dialogue is used:

1. To reveal character

No two people are exactly alike. No two people, given the same stimulus, will speak exactly alike. When you meet a stranger for the first time you *see* him. From his physical appearance you form an impression of him. He may give the impression of being a tough egg, but tough-looking eggs have been known to have hearts of gold. When your stranger speaks, however, his true character begins to emerge. He *is* tough. His speech is coarse, vulgar, belligerent, even threatening. There you have one character. If, on the other hand, despite his looks, his speech reveals him to have a heart of gold you have an entirely different character. By means of dialogue you can also characterize a character other than your protagonist. For example:

> "What a witch that Marge Evans is," Sarah said indignantly. "Why, she even looks like one, with her scraggly hair and the long black dresses she wears. And the way she treats that child of hers. She doesn't just spank him, she beats him."

2. To show the speaker's emotions

People under stress do not talk the same as when they are merely in conversation about the weather. If your protagonist is angry, make him sound angry. Use angry words. If he is being sarcastic, let his speech be sarcastic. If he's indignant, let his indignation show in every word he utters. By showing emotion through dialogue you are also revealing character. A character may seem one person under tranquil conditions; under stress, through his dialogue, he may reveal himself basically to be an entirely different person.

3. To give information

Way back in the dark ages of my writing career I used to narrate information into my stories. I would bring the action of my stories to a dead stop while I told the reader all about my characters, where they were born, how they grew up, what they were doing. It was only one of a thousand mistakes I was making, but it was one of the more serious, and it took me years to overcome it. Today I use narration very sparingly, usually for the sake of variety. I rely mostly on dialogue to get across whatever information I'm trying to weave into my stories. We'll come to examples of this in a minute.

4. To bring out the conflict

Suppose you have two men in a room. They glare at each other. They walk around the room, waving their arms angrily. Finally they start fighting. You don't know what about. The whole thing looks rather silly, and futile. But let them speak, let the conflict between them erupt in words, and there's nothing silly about it. Characters come alive; emotions are aroused, the conflict is not only revealed, it is intensified many times over. The wheels of creation are turning and the action of our story and the development of our plot are moving forward again. In the pantomime scene our story was churning, getting nowhere.

5. To build suspense

You see this technique constantly used on television. The villain says, "I'll get you for this. I'll kill you if you're not out of town by sunset." Or the hero says, "I don't like those clouds over there. Looks to me like a tornado coming, and the nearest storm cellar is ten miles away." Or the heroine says, "I'm afraid of Jack. He's been acting strangely lately. I think he means to harm me." A promise of danger, or disaster, or heightened conflict in each case is foreshadowed. The reader reads on to see what will happen.

6. To tie up the loose ends of your story

Very often in detective stories much of what has happened is summed up at the end in a page, or in several pages, of dialogue. In any other type of story, it is best to use this technique very sparingly. The average reader doesn't like to have characters tell what has happened. They prefer to see the story unfold dramatically before their eyes. If this has been done, it eliminates the necessity of a summation. However, if the fate of a character is left dangling, and you don't want to bring him on scene again, you can disclose it through the dialogue of others. This is permissible, too, for tying up any loose ends of information. Just make it brief.

The dynamic approach

Here are some examples of how these points of technique were used in published stories. This is from the same story mentioned in the previous chapter on characterization. Pete is a young ex-soldier. While on overseas duty, he receives a "Dear John" letter from his best girl, giving him the pitch. He has promised Brody, his top sergeant, never again to take a girl seriously. At the story opening, you'll remember, he is making a living on a Florida beach by taking pictures of tourists on a live ox. A girl and her male companion in the sand sailer have run into his ox, knocking him down and upsetting the sailer. Pete has helped the girl and her companion crawl from under the sailer. Through Pete's eyes we have described the girl. Then:

> There was a skinned place on her shoulder and a scratch on her skin but she ignored these and inquired anxiously, "Is your friend all right?"

Over her shoulder old Brody's face was peering at him anxiously and Pete said, "My friend is delicate and easily bruised; especially when run over by freight trains and sail boats."

She walked past him and sank to her knees beside Ferdinand. "I'm Alice Reed and I'm so sorry I ran into you. I hope you're not hurt?"

Pete knelt beside her and when he looked at her he could hear old Brody's voice talking to him soothingly back in Korea, "Whenever you meet a girl just keep it all in fun, kid, and you'll be all right."

"Miss Reed, Mr. Ferdinand; and I'm Pete Miller," he said.

"How do you do." Alice included them both in her nod. "I'm worried about your friend. Shouldn't you do something?"

Pete felt Ferdinand's pulse. "It *is* a little weak."

"Seriously," she insisted.

"If you'll hold his hoof and comfort him I'll call an ambulance," he said.

This is a light love story and the problem and conflict are, consequently, not ones of mayhem and rape. But conflict there is in this story; in fact, there are two conflicts. One is Pete's inner conflict over girls. He has been badly burned, and he has old Brody's advice (this is his motivation in the story), but he is attracted toward Alice in a very disturbing way. The second conflict, which we'll show in a minute, is with the villain, Alice's sailing companion. In this first passage, both Pete and Alice have also been characterized. They are nice people, pleasant, interesting. From their good-humored banter, the reader grows to like them, and thus an emotion is aroused within him. In Pete's thoughts of old Brody, information is given the reader, too, by means of dialogue. Brody's dialogue also serves to establish firmly the inner conflict. Not one but several functions have been performed by this piece of dialogue. If this were not so, *it would have no place in the story.*

Here's the conflict, by means of dialogue, starting between Pete and the villain, Alice's friend:

> They were interrupted by a blond Nordic-looking giant who had crawled out from under the sailer and was regarding them disgustedly. "That cow isn't half as sick as this wreck."
>
> Alice and Pete stood up and Alice introduced the young man as Harry Moore, down from New York on his vacation.
>
> "Ox," Pete said.
>
> "What's the difference?" Harry Moore said. "And what's it doing on the beach anyway?"
>
> Pete didn't like that question. "Trying to mind its own business."
>
> "There should be a law against turning the beach into a cow pasture."
>
> "I think we'd better be going." Alice stepped between them hastily. She smiled at Pete. "I hope Mr. Ferdinand will be all right."

We have thus characterized Harry Moore as being a disagreeable sort of person, and we have aroused an emotion of dislike in the reader. The second conflict has been brought out, the story action advanced, and suspense created. Again the dialogue has performed more than one function.

Here's an example to show how trouble was foreshadowed and suspense built. Ann is at the railroad station meeting her husband, Bill, who is returning from two years in prison. The villain, Dana Reese, has brutally killed Bill's dog. Perk Munson, a friend and neighbor, warns Ann:

"Dana Reese has bought a gun, Ann."

A shiver ran through Ann and she covered her mouth with one hand.

"I'm telling you, you'd better get Bill away from Scottsville," Perk went on excitedly. "The old trouble between him and Reese was bad enough, but it wasn't anything compared to this. Bill won't hesitate when he learns the truth. And you can bet your bottom dollar someone in this town will tell him."

This could have been brought out in Ann's thinking or in narrative, but it would have been flat, lifeless, and weak. Dialogue gave it the necessary sense of urgency. It moved the plot forward, gave some necessary information about Bill as well.

Here's another example:

All at once Jimmy wanted to talk about himself. He wanted to tell about his face. "It was in a fire," he said abruptly. "Our house caught in the night when everyone was asleep. I remember waking up and trying to get out, but the smoke made me sick. The last thing I knew a beam fell on me. A neighbor dragged me out."

"What about your folks?" Randall asked.

Jimmy shook his head.

Randall was silent a moment. "How old're you, son?"

"Seventeen."

"What do you do?"

"Odd jobs."

"Just drifting?"

Jimmy shrugged.

"Why?" The speculative look was in the old man's eyes again.

Jimmy looked up and couldn't keep the bitterness from his voice. "You got eyes."

"So what?"

Jimmy turned toward Randall, showing the side of his face that had been burned. "That," he said bitterly. He pointed to the scar cutting across his mouth from nose to chin. "And that." He turned the other side of his face so Randall could see it. "And that."

Randall pursed his lips. "Maybe a lot of it's just in your head."

Jimmy didn't answer.

The chief reason for writing this scene was to bring out the information about Jimmy's face, and to let the reader see it in a dramatic way. It could have been done by narrative, but then it would have been dull, and undramatic. There would have been no emotion, no conflict, no forward movement to the story, no characterization. By using dialogue, we arouse in the reader a feeling of sympathy for Jimmy. Jimmy's own emotional reaction has been shown and transmitted to the reader. Something of Jimmy's background and character has been revealed, and this inner conflict, his struggle to accept his affliction, has been established. Again, not one, but many, functions have been performed by the use of dialogue. I keep stressing this point, because it's so important for the writing of *salable* fiction.

Now we come to an example of dialogue that performs only one function:

Bill was carrying an inner tube. "I can't swim," he apologized.

"I didn't think there was anyone over the age of six months who couldn't," Peg marvelled.

"I come from a part of Texas that never saw more than a glassful of water at a time."

She was looking at him curiously. "Your family lives in Texas?"

"An uncle," Bill answered. "My parents were killed in a tornado when I was a kid."

"Oh," Peg said. Then she added. "My mother died when I was born."

This dialogue tells us something of the background of the two characters, Bill and Peg, but notice that it is very brief. To continue it any further would have been fatal. It would have become both boring and irritating to the reader.

We have discussed the many functions of dialogue. Here, in conclusion, is one very important rule. Make your dialogue sound natural. Make it fit the character, and never allow it to become stilted. For instance, two teen-agers meeting at the drugstore after school would not talk like this:

"How are you, Henry? I understand that Mary has declined your invitation to the dance tonight and is being escorted instead by William Fosdick."

"That is so," Henry agreed solemnly.

That may sound farfetched, but it isn't. I've read many passages by beginners as stilted as this. To make it more natural we could write:

"Hyah, Hank. What's this rumble I hear about Mary going to the dance tonight with Bill Fosdick instead of you?"

"The rumble does not lie." Hank put his hand over his heart dramatically. He tried to make the words sound light, unconcerned. "She cut out, man."

Dialogue is one of the most useful tools of fiction technique, simply because it can perform so many functions. Use it at every opportunity. It brings your characters to life. And living, breathing, interesting characters are what the editors are continually searching for in stories.

₰ 8

HOW TO DRAMATIZE YOUR STORY

MANY PROFESSIONAL WRITERS use a great deal of narration in their stories. By narration we simply mean that setting, characterization, sensory appeal, sometimes dialogue, and many of the other elements of technique, are presented by means of *telling*. A character, for example, is *described* by the author. The reader is *told* what sort of person the character is, what he looks like, what clothing he is wearing.

Many other professional writers rely heavily on dramatization to put their stories across. By dramatization we mean that setting, characterization, etc., are presented by means of *showing*. A character, for example, is developed through *action*.

Of the two, dramatization and narration, dramatization is by far the most difficult to do. It is the purpose of this chapter, therefore, to show how a professional makes use of dramatization. Let's take six of the elements of technique and show how they can be presented dramatically, instead of by narration. We'll show how we can turn narration into dramatization.

Dialogue

Not so long ago I was asked to read a story and the dialogue ran pretty much like this:

> John found Mary in the library. He told her harshly that he was leaving. When she fearfully asked him why, he said he didn't love her any more. Shocked, she asked him if there was somebody else? He said, no.

This is narration at its worst. If an editor were to read it he would probably become ill. So let's take pity on him and give it some life. Let's dramatize it:

> Mary put her back to the fireplace. It was as though she were bracing herself for the shock she knew was coming.
>
> John looked around the library, their library for ten years, and, for a moment, he felt misgivings. Then a harsh voice he hardly recognized as his own said, "I'm leaving, Mary. Today. Now."
>
> He hadn't meant to be harsh. He saw the fear spring into her eyes. He saw her face turn pale.
>
> "Why?" Her voice was barely audible.
>
> John drew in his breath sharply. He'd known that would be her first question and he had only one answer. "I don't love you any more."
>
> Now he saw the shock in her face, and in her eyes.
>
> "Is there someone else?" she whispered.
>
> John shook his head. "No."

And so we have dramatized, instead of narrated, the dialogue. We, the author, haven't *told* what the characters said. We have let the characters *speak for themselves*. We have also dramatized both characters' reactions; but we will go into that more fully in a moment.

Characterization

I often give a brief physical description of my protagonist at the opening of a story, then dramatize his "whole" character throughout the body of the story. Here's an example:

> Bill was a tall, blond young man in shorts and a striped jersey, and his skin was the burned red of a week-old Floridian's. He had blue eyes and a peeling nose, and his mouth was wide—usually smiling.

This is straight narration. Now let's dramatize the same material:

> Bill eased his long frame down onto his blanket and brushed the sand from his shorts and striped jersey. His blue eyes idly watched a girl walking up the beach toward him.

This is about as much as we can dramatize his physical appearance at one time—without being too obvious about what we're doing, and without making him move his hands and arms around like a marionette. Suppose he speaks to the girl, and she gives him the brush-off. Now we can write:

> Bill ran his fingers through his blond hair ruefully and shrugged. Maybe she wasn't the type who talked to strange men—he hoped. Or maybe he was a worse sight than he'd thought, with his peeling nose and skin the burned red of a week-old Floridian's. His wide mouth—usually smiling —drooped disappointedly as he watched her walk away.

We have described Bill dramatically, in action, using action verbs instead of the inactive verbs, "was," and, "had." Since thoughts are action, and dramatic, we used them in two sentences to show his peeling nose and sun-burned skin.

Here's an example of a *character trait*. First let's narrate it:

Henry was lazy.

Now let's dramatize it in action:

Henry crossed the street, each dragging step groaning with resentment at the energy wasted.

The following is another example of a character trait, first narrated, then dramatized:

David had a temper.
David's eyes blazed with sudden uncontrolled fury.

See what a difference it makes? See how a character springs to life when his traits and characteristics are dramatized instead of narrated?

Physical reaction

By means of reaction, we reveal a character's emotional state, his emotional response to a stimulus. We do this with dialogue, thought, and physical reactions. We have shown how to dramatize dialogue. Here is an example of a physical reaction, first narrated, then dramatized:

Oscar was nervous.
Oscar hunched forward onto the edge of his seat. His fingers toyed with the brim of his hat. He was sweating suddenly.

Here's another example:

Mary was frightened.
Mary clamped both hands over her mouth. She could

feel her heart beating wildly, and the fear—the terror—rising like gall into her throat.

Again in this we have eliminated the verb "was," and substituted action verbs. We have dramatized, or acted out, the reactions, not told them. And by doing so we have aroused an emotion within the character, and within the reader.

Sensory appeal

If we were to write, "The apple tasted sour to Larry," we would be making a simple statement of fact. We would be telling the reader that the apple tasted sour to Larry. How can we dramatize it? Let's do it with action, and dialogue.

> Larry spat out the piece of apple. "Wow!" He grimaced. "That's a sour one!"

You can count on one thing: All readers are "from Missouri." They won't believe anything that is told them. In this case they want to taste the apple for themselves. Let them experience the sense of smell, through a character. Instead of, "Old man Sewell smelled bad," let's say:

> When old man Sewell slouched into the room Bill rose quickly and stood by the open window. What pig pen, he thought desperately, had the old fellow been wallowing in now? Or rather, Bill thought guiltily, what neighborhood garbage pail had he been eating out of last? Old man Sewell smelled sickeningly today of rancid grease and spoiled food.

Setting

Sometimes in short stories and more often in novels you find long passages of setting, or scenery, *as told by the author.* This is narration, and is perfectly permissible, if interestingly done. But what if the writer wants to dramatize it? *All he has to do is show the setting through the main character's eyes.* Don't forget that the reader wants to identify himself with the protagonist; he wants to live the story with the protagonist; he wants to see the setting as the protagonist sees it. Here's an example of how this is done:

> Jimmy looked out over the fence at the grandstands. Workmen were decorating it with flags and bunting, and concessionaires were setting up their booths in preparation for the opening of the rodeo tomorrow. There was the sound of hammers, a voice blared briefly over a loudspeaker, and from the corrals and stables beyond the chutes came the bawling of cattle and the occasional whinny of a horse.

Here we have set the scene of a rodeo grounds. We have used the sensory appeals of sight and sound to do this. And we have done it through Jimmy's eyes—"Jimmy looked out over the fence at the grandstands." By leading off with this single sentence we draw the reader into the story. He sees what Jimmy sees, hears what Jimmy hears. Without that lead sentence the description of the rodeo grounds would be straight author telling.

In the next example, we've put the protagonist in a carriage driving into a strange town. This puts him, *and* the reader, on scene. In the second sentence, we inject, "Glenn saw," to make absolutely sure that the reader identifies himself with the protagonist and sees the setting through his eyes.

Their carriage started up and swung into the procession of vehicles entering the town from the levee and the steamboat landing. North and south for half a mile in either direction, and west for nearly the same distance, Chickasaw, Glenn saw, was a bustling, rowdy frontier and river town. Its buildings, some of them along the main street, were imposing, but for the most part were shacks. Its streets were dusty in dry weather and muddy in wet. The weather had been hot and dry, and now the Kimlockes drove through a thick haze of dust kicked up by the horses of other carriages.

Their coachman picked his way carefully through the center of town, crowded with carriages like their own and wagons of every description and size, from light buggies to great lumbering freighters plodding through to the levee. The board sidewalks built along both sides of the street were crowded, even in the heat of the day. There were rough, burly teamsters, and fancily-dressed gentlemen; and women in sunbonnets and women in silk and lace, carrying parasols against the sun's rays. There was noise in the streets, the rattle of wheels, voices, the loud discordant sound of a man singing drunkenly on the steps of a saloon.

Notice that this bit of setting was broken up into two paragraphs to keep it from becoming monotonous; and that the second, as well as the first, leads off with action; the first to draw, the second to hold, the reader on scene. You have probably already noticed that in the body of both paragraphs the inactive verbs "was" and "had" are used. This is not the best technique, but it is permissible when reader identification has been established, when the reader has been brought on scene, and when the setting is described through the protagonist's eyes. It is also permissible when additional setting is to be shown in action.

Thoughts

The same procedure is followed with thought reactions as with setting. Lead off with the protagonist performing some action, then go into his thoughts. The thoughts then are his. They spring from his mind. Take away the action sentence and the thoughts are told, or narrated, by the author. For example:

> Bill sank onto the orange crate and didn't answer right away. He'd known there would be opposition, plenty of it, but he still didn't quite know how to meet it. The trouble was that he was too much in love with Vivian Warren, and had been ever since she'd shown up at the hospital that first day.

The lead sentence of this paragraph makes it Bill's paragraph. The thoughts that follow are automatically identified as his, as coming from him. If you take away this lead sentence and start with, "Bill had known—," you will see how it becomes straight author telling Bill's thoughts. Here's another example:

> Ann shivered. There was one night in particular Bill must never learn about. That was the night Dan Warren had tried to break into the house and had gone away only when he'd heard her frantically telephoning for the police.

"Ann shivered." These two words of action are all it took to change a paragraph from narration to dramatization, to *show* a character's thoughts, instead of *telling* them.

9

HOW TO PLOT YOUR STORY

PLOTTING A STORY is *the* big bugaboo of most beginning writers. It was mine, and it took about two million words of floundering before I began to get a glimmer of what it was all about. I'd like to save you those two million words (and those hundreds, no thousands, of rejection slips) and tell you all that I have learned about this business of plotting. For years I studied published stories, and read all the books on writing that I could lay my hands on, but still the meaning of plot eluded me. It eluded me until I learned one simple, basic fact:

Plot is drama. Or, to put it differently, *plot is non-existent in a story unless there is drama.*

How does one plot a dramatic story? Let's go back and start from scratch. In planning a story, I try to arrange my material so that it has a beginning, a middle, and an end. In a twenty-page story, I allot roughly five or six pages to my beginning, twelve or fourteen pages to my middle, and one or two to my ending. I say roughly because there is no set rule on this.

The idea for my story can spring from one of many sources—from a character, or a situation, or an unusual setting. The next step is to take my protagonist and give him a problem to resolve. Once I have done this, I think up an opening scene that will reveal the problem to the reader. I try to do this on the first page. I try to bring my protagonist into immediate conflict with his problem, which may be a struggle within himself, a struggle with another character, a struggle with nature, or a combination of two or three of these. If I am unable to reveal the problem in the first page, I try to reveal it at least by the end of the beginning section of my story. By the end of my beginning, I also start my protagonist out on the road to resolving his problem.

In my floundering days, I would at this point plan the middle part of my story. I would lay out the course of action my protagonist would take toward resolving his problem at the climax. It was hard, gruelling, and discouraging work, and nine times out of ten I would fail and throw the whole idea away. Why was it such a task? Simply because I didn't know where I was going. I was groping blindly in the dark.

I wasted years trying to figure a way out of this predicament, but eventually I found one so simple I haven't stopped kicking myself yet for not thinking of it sooner. After stating the problem fully in the beginning section of my story, I now jump to the climax and figure out the resolution. When I have done this, I go back and fill in the middle section. It makes plotting far simpler. I can now control my story action, instead of having it fly off willy-nilly in ten different directions at once. I can give it unity and direction, and I can more fully develop plants and foreshadowing.

Obstacle, struggle, crisis

We have said that the protagonist must start working on his problem by the end of the beginning section of the story, and that he must resolve his problem in twelve or fourteen pages. This is where the fun comes in—to make it just as rough on him as we possibly can. We do this by throwing obstacles in his path. We do not throw him easy ones that he can overcome. We throw him tough ones that overcome *him*. Each time he tries to overcome an obstacle, the action and emotion rise to a crisis. He fails in his attempt, the crisis passes, the action and the emotion fall, and the scene ends. In the next scene the process is repeated. The formula for this process we might say then is this: The bigger the obstacle, the greater the struggle; the more intense the crisis, the deeper the gap between the rise and fall in action. Weak obstacles reverse this process. They can only result in a weak story.

Let's take some scenes and fit them into the sections of a story. Let's take a story of five scenes and put one in the *beginning*, three in the *middle* or *body*, and one in the *end*. We have already said that in the *beginning* we fully state the problem and start the protagonist to work solving it. We have also said that in the *middle*, we throw obstacles in the protagonist's path, strong ones that will raise the action and emotional levels to points of intense crisis. In a three-scene *middle* we have three such crises. The first two are minor, the third is major.

We can compare them to three knockdowns in a prize fight. In the first two, the protagonist is brought to his knees; in the third he is flattened for the count of nine. In the first two knockdowns, he is staggered, but the crowd can see that he will be able to get up and continue the fight. In the third knockdown, he is only half conscious, in a fog, and the crowd despairs, thinking he won't be able to make it. But at the count of nine he gets to his feet and goes on to win the fight.

At the point when our protagonist is down it looks as though he has lost the fight. All seems lost. This is called the Black Moment. This Black Moment precipitates a Crisis which, in turn, forces the protagonist to make a Decision. He must decide whether he is going to lie still and accept defeat, or whether he will get up and go on fighting. He doesn't ever think about it. He doesn't ever think, or say out loud, "I've got to get up and fight." But he gets up and knocks out his opponent. This is the climax of the story. The protagonist has taken action to solve his problem. The *middle* section of the story is over. In the end section, the protagonist is acclaimed the winner. The reader is left with a feeling of satisfaction at the way things have turned out.

There are two types of stories. One is the plotted type. The other is the formless type. The formless type stresses character and is usually a "slice of life" story. The plotted type follows a planned course toward a dramatic climax. We are concerned with the plotted story here, because in the past, and probably for a long time to come, it is the most sought after by many magazines, television, and the movies.

Plot patterns

There are definite patterns into which all plotted stories fall. These patterns are classic and have been used down through the ages.*

The first of the patterns that we'll discuss here is the story of *Purpose Accomplishment*. This pattern is the most commonly used in fiction. The protagonist has a problem to resolve or a purpose to accomplish. In the end he triumphs. The prize fighter story is a good example of this pattern. The protagonist is beaten down by obstacles, but hurdles the biggest obstacle of all, the Black Moment, when he is on the canvas, and wins. What is an obstacle? It is anything that threatens to stop him from accomplishing his purpose.

We know that every story must have conflict. Let's give our prize fighter three conflicts. He is, of course, in conflict with his adversary in the ring. He can also be in conflict with his adversary outside the ring, before the big fight. His adversary can be making a play for his best girl.

The second conflict can be with his girl. Suppose our protagonist is old (for a fighter) and tired, that he is only fighting because he desperately needs the money so he can marry the girl. But, not understanding the age (he need only be in his thirties) factor in fighting, she thinks he is a quitter. She accuses him of it. They argue.

The third conflict is within himself. He gives such a

---

* A very comprehensive study of patterns can be found in John Gallishaw's book, *Twenty Problems of the Fiction Writer.*

poor showing during his training period that he begins to think his girl is right, that maybe he *is* a quitter. He loses faith in himself and has to fight against this feeling.

One conflict is seldom enough to sustain a story. Two man-against-man conflicts (one a woman in this case) make a better story. Adding the third, man against himself, gives the story depth. All three story lines run parallel to each other until the climax, at which point solving any one conflict will automatically resolve the other two.

Come-to-realize plots

Now let's look at the next story pattern. This is the story of *Purpose Abandonment*. It is known more commonly as the Come-to-Realize pattern and is found mostly in the women's magazines. Its structure is similar to that of the Purpose Accomplishment pattern in every respect but two. In the body of the story of Accomplishment, the protagonist has obstacles that keep him from reaching his goal. In the Abandonment story, there are no such obstacles. The protagonist's every effort meets with success.

The Abandonment story differs from the Achievement story, too, at the climax, in that the protagonist abandons his purpose instead of accomplishing it. He abandons it when he sees that accomplishment will only bring unhappiness to himself and/or others. From the opening line to the climax of the story, the protagonist never wavers in his determination to accomplish what he has set out to do. He does not see that achievement will bring unhappiness or greater unhappiness, *but the reader does* and hopes that the protagonist will give up his purpose before it is too late. Having the reader see, and the protagonist not see, this threat of unhappiness, builds suspense. The suspense reaches its peak when the protagonist has the achievement of his purpose within his reach. All he has to do is grab it, and it is his. This is *his* Bright Moment, because success is his, but it is the reader's Black Moment, because he does not want the protagonist to have it.

But at this point a *New Force* enters the picture. This results in a *Crisis* that forces the protagonist to make a *Decision*. Because of the New Force, he decides to abandon his purpose. His abandonment is the Climax, or the Come-to-Realize, of the story. The Climax and the Come-to-Realize in the abandonment story are one and the same thing. The protagonist comes to realize that he no longer wants to achieve his purpose.

For example, a young wife wants to divorce her husband who is an incurable gambler. When they were married, she was young and blindly in love with him. She knew he gambled, but she overlooked it. She saw only his good qualities. He was kind, easy-going, and good-natured, and she loved him for these qualities. She didn't take the gambling seriously. She thought she could easily change him, in fact that he would change, out of equal love for her. But in ten years she hasn't changed him. To make matters worse, he is not a successful gambler. A goodly portion of his salary as a bank teller he loses each week. He is continually in debt, and his family (they have two children) are kept in semi-pauperism. The wife reaches a point where she has had enough. She wants a divorce. This is her purpose in the story.

The story opens one morning when she is getting her husband's suit ready to take to the cleaners. When she goes through his pockets to make sure there is nothing in them, she finds some racing ticket stubs. This shocks her because only a few days before he had promised to stop gambling. She goes to a lawyer and tells him the whole story. He says she can get her divorce if she can furnish proof and a witness. She goes home and makes up a balance sheet, comparing his salary with their expenses. That shows how much he has spent gambling. It is even more than she has thought, and she becomes more determined than ever to get a divorce.

She goes next to see her neighbor whose husband has accompanied her husband on some of his gambling jaunts. The neighbor is glad to testify. That evening the wife sends the children out into the yard to play. When her husband comes home, she tells him that she has something she wants to discuss with him. But at that moment the children come running into the house. They give their father a big welcome, want him to come out and see a tree house they are building. Eager and excited, they each take him by a hand and lead him from the house. Through the window the wife watches him admiring their tree. He even climbs the tree and sits in it with them. When he comes back into the house, he asks the wife, "What did you want to tell me?" Her answer is, "Nothing."

The wife's Bright Moment—and the reader's Black Moment—is when she informs her husband that she has something to tell him. She has her purpose in the palm of her hand. The New Force is the children. They bring on the Crisis, which forces her to make a Decision (automatically and without thought or dialogue). The Climax comes when she says, "Nothing." She abandons her purpose, and simultaneously Comes-to-Realize. Now, but not before this point in the story, she can think, or come to realize, how much the children love their father, and how much *more* unhappiness she would cause for them all if she were to go through with the divorce. She begins to see again in her husband the traits she loved in him at the time of their marriage, but these had become overshadowed of late by his persistent gambling habits. The story does not end in complete happiness for her. It does end, however, on a happier note than at the opening. His good qualities seem now to compensate somewhat for his gambling.

Stories of decision

We come now to the third story pattern. This is the story of *Decision*. In this pattern, the protagonist has to choose between two courses of action, one good for him, the other bad. But—and it is very important that this is thoroughly understood—he does not know which choice is good and which is bad. The reader *does* know, however, and suspense is created each time the protagonist leans toward the wrong choice. And lean he does. He sways from one choice to the other, perhaps half a dozen times throughout the story. This swaying is what distinguishes the Decision story from the story of Purpose Abandonment in which the protagonist never once swerves from his intended purpose. Near the climax, he leans sharply toward the wrong choice. This is the reader's Black Moment. At this point, a New Force appears that brings on the Crisis. This Crisis demands that a Decision, or choice, be made. The Decision *is* made, and this decision becomes the Climax of the story.

As an example, let's rework the divorce story into a Decision story. The wife now does not have a purpose to accomplish. She has a decision to make: She has to decide whether or not she will divorce her husband. She is fully aware of his good traits and is equally aware of the children's love for him and what divorce will do to them. But she can't take any more of his gambling. She is torn. At the end, when she finds the racing tickets, she leans sharply toward divorce. This is the reader's Black Moment. The New Force enters here, in the form of a note she finds on his dresser table. It's to her from her husband. It simply states that he knows she is contemplating divorce and that he is leaving. We are now at the Crisis. In a panic, she runs from the house, grabs a taxi, and goes to the bank where he works. This is the Climax of the story. She has made her decision. Gambler or no gambler she can't bear the thought of losing him. She wants him back. To all intent and purpose the story is now over, but we could give it a happier ending by having the husband promise that he will stop gambling. She knows that gambling to him is like liquor to an alcoholic, and she desperately hopes he *will* stop, but the important thing now is having him come home. By nearly losing him she has discovered how much she loves him.

The fourth pattern is known as the Biter-Bit pattern. It is the only pattern in which the protagonist is *always* the villain. His purpose is always to hurt some innocent, unsuspecting, and good, person. But he does not achieve his purpose. In the end he fails. Now here is why this pattern is called Biter-Bit: *He fails in his purpose by his own act, not by some force beyond his control.*

Let's give an example of this pattern. The protagonist is a gangster. A private detective has found evidence of his gangsterism that will send him to jail, and he decides to take the detective for a "ride." He walks into the detective's office one day and says, "Let's go." He has a gun in his coat pocket, and he warns the detective he will kill him instantly if he talks to anyone on the way out. They leave the office, and the elevator boy says hello to the detective. The detective answers hello briefly in reply. On the corner a newsboy tries to sell the detective a paper, but the detective shakes his head and walks on. Further on, a shoeshine boy wants to shine the detective's shoes. The detective doesn't answer. He and the gangster get into the gangster's car and drive away.

But half a mile away a police car stops them, and the gangster is arrested. It is revealed then that the detective is a very friendly guy. In the past he has always chatted with the elevator boy; he has always, every morning, bought a newspaper from the newsboy; he has always had the shoeshine boy shine his shoes. When he snubbed them, they suspected something was wrong and called the police. Thus the villain is trapped by his own act.

The Biter-Bit pattern is very seldom used in long stories. Interest and suspense are too difficult to sustain. It is usually used in short-shorts in magazines that cater to readers who prefer stories of action rather than character.

These are the four patterns. We have discussed their structure, but I would like to clarify more fully one point. This is the Come-to-Realize. It is possible to find a Come-to-Realize in all of the first three types, and this is sometimes confusing. It is found, of course, in all Come-to-Realize or Purpose Abandonment stories. But it can also be found in the Purpose Accomplishment story, whenever there is a character, or man-against-himself problem. The protagonist can "come to realize" his character flaw in his thinking or in a *brief* passage of dialogue. This *come-to-realize* is always found in the End section of the story, *after* the climax, *never before* it. Putting it *before* the climax kills all drama.

In the Purpose Abandonment story, the *come-to-realize* is, of course, an essential part of the structure. It is the climax. Without it there is no story. In the Decision story, it appears in the End section, *after* the decision has been made. In the example given earlier, the Decision comes at the point when the wife abandons divorce; and *comes-to-realize* when she realizes how much she needs, and loves, her husband.

In conclusion I would like to make still one more point clear. Improper sequence in presenting the various elements at the climax will invariably result in a weak, plotless story. Having the *come-to-realize* come before the climax is an example. But if you follow the proper sequence your story will have *drama*. And *drama,* as we have said earlier, *is plot.*

~~ 10

LET'S BUILD A STORY

INSTEAD OF OUTLINING and discussing the technique of building a story, let's actually build one, step by step, from the original idea to the final paragraph. I've done this many times in fiction writing classes I have taught, and it always seemed to help clarify the business of plotting.

The first step, of course, is to find something to write about. When I'm working on one story, I always try to keep two or three others working in the back of my mind. This gives me a feeling of security. Many times I've finished a story only to find myself without ideas, and it's rather a frightening state to be in. Intellectually, I know that with more than twenty-five years of writing experience behind me, I'll come up with an idea sooner or later, but emotionally I feel at that moment that I'll never be able to think of one again.

All I need is an incident, a character, a conflict, to start the plot wheels rolling. Here's an incident that kicked around in my mind for years. It's just an incident, but let's see how we can build a story around it. When my neighbor's daughter was about fourteen years old, her school class made a trip to St. Augustine, Florida, to see all the historical sights, Ye Old Fort, Ye Old School House, Ye Old Arch, etc. That night she staggered into the house with a souvenir of her trip, a three-hundred-year-old, twenty-five-pound cannon ball she'd swiped from Ye Oldest House. Her father lectured her on taking things that didn't belong to her and told her that it must be returned. He didn't have the heart to make her take it back, so he drove up to St. Augustine the next day and returned it himself. He didn't quite dare walk into Ye Oldest House with it, so he drove slowly by, opened the car door and rolled it, like a billiard ball, through the door. The proprietor must have been startled when it came rolling through his door, but my neighbor didn't wait to see.

Years ago I would have written the story just as it happened, then wondered why it didn't sell. As we have said, it's only an incident and can be used only as such, perhaps for our opening.

Let's use it for the opening. We must decide from whose viewpoint the story will be told. The father's? No. So many stories have been written about parents dealing with children's problems that I shy away from them. The daughter's? Again, no, for the same reason. But how about telling it from the daughter's viewpoint, making her five years older? That's better. Now the idea is wide open with possibilities. Now we can introduce romance into the story, and romance is always a good bet.

What next? Is the nineteen-year-old girl going to be the one to swipe the cannon ball? I think she's too old for such things. It would make it an out-and-out theft, instead of a kid prank. No, it will have to be someone younger, preferably a boy, cannon balls being more suited to a boy. But the nineteen-year-old girl is too young to have children. Can it be a brother, then? Why not? But wouldn't it be unlikely for a sister to be handling the situation? Isn't it the father's or mother's job? It is; but suppose the boy doesn't have any parents?

Here we go. Suppose the parents are dead, and the older sister is bringing up the boy? Let's give her a brother *and* a sister, for good measure. Now we have the start of a problem. It's no easy trick for a nineteen-year-old girl to bring up two lively youngsters. But here we run into some obstacles. Would the courts allow it? Would she be able to swing it financially?

To get around the legal end of it is a stumper, but there's a way. Let's bring in an aunt who needs a home. She moves in with them, and the court now allows the older sister to keep and raise the children. The aunt also has a small pension which helps out on the finances. The older sister, let's call her Sally, has to work because her father left his family a house but no money. Why was he so poor? Since most college professors barely earn a living, let's make him one. This gives us our setting, a college town. Let's make Sally a part-time student.

What do we have thus far? We have a nineteen-year-old girl struggling to finish college and at the same time raise two children on a limited budget. That's quite a job, but she tackles it with courage, which makes her a sympathetic character. We also have our setting. So far so good.

How about her romance? Her second problem should center around this. She should fall in love with someone, and then have a hard time nailing him. We can make him one of her teachers, but that's sort of commonplace. It's better if we make him a fellow student. Not another nineteen-year-old, though. That would give us a story about teen-agers, and would lessen our chances of a sale. Let's make him older, twenty-three or four, a young fellow doing post-graduate work for his master's degree.

That's pretty good. Now all we have to do is somehow tie his post-graduate work in with Sally's problem of raising two children. This will give our story unity. But what can he be studying? Animal husbandry? Archaeology? Biology? There's no tie-in with any of these, so out the window they go.

How about making him a sociology student? How about having him write his thesis around Sally and her family? This brings him in contact with her daily, and quite naturally. It also gives us a chance to build up conflict between them. She is in love with him but thinks his interest in her is only because of his thesis. That means that for some reason he must hold himself aloof from her. If he declares his love for her at the very beginning, they'll simply fall into each other's arms, and the story will end before it even gets started.

Here's a possible solution: Somewhere in the story have Sally state that she wishes she had a million dollars. The boy—we'll call him Bill—loves Sally very much, but after her remark he hides his love from her because he knows he'll never be anything but a poor teacher, unable to give her even a small fraction of her million dollars. We can let Bill be aloof because he thinks he's too poor for her, and let Sally be hurt because she thinks his interest is purely academic. We can hold back on the question of finances until the very end.

The opening scene

Now we're about ready to figure out an opening for the story, utilizing, of course, the incident of the cannon ball. Since Sally is the protagonist, we'll let her return the cannon ball to its rightful place beside two Civil War cannons standing in the center of the college campus. We want to bring Sally and Bill together on scene as quickly as possible. It's dusk and she hurries across the campus, lugging the cannon ball wrapped in a paper bag. She drops it beside the cannon, but as she turns to leave, she sees Bill sitting at the base of a statue, watching her. They've met before, in the library where she works part-time, and she's already a little in love with him. He is curious about the cannon ball, and she tells him about it and about her "children." He walks her home. He meets the children and Aunt Martha, and then he and Sally sit on the porch and talk. Sally thinks he has walked her home because he is interested in *her,* and she is thrilled and flattered. Then suddenly he tells her that he has started a thesis, but it isn't going too well. He would like to drop it and start another—built around her and the children. Reluctantly she gives her permission, and he leaves. She is hurt, crushed.

So ends the first scene. We have opened with a narrative hook (the cannon ball incident), introduced all the characters in the story, set the scene, established the emotional tone, characterized the two principal actors, and stated the two problems: Sally's struggle to raise her family, and her love for Bill. The action has risen to a crisis and fallen. Now we're ready to start the second scene.

But first (as we've stated in the chapter on plot) we must go to the climax of the story and figure out solutions to the two problems. Let's take Sally's love problem first. But wait a minute. We've forgotten something. We haven't decided what pattern we're going to use. We should have decided that long ago. It's not a Biter-Bit. It's not a Decision story; she doesn't choose between two courses of action; she's simply in love with Bill. Neither is it an Abandonment story. She doesn't abandon anything.

It has to be an Accomplishment story. What are the steps to be taken at the climax of an accomplishment story? First of all, there's the Black Moment. Sally is in conflict with Bill throughout the story, as she falls more deeply in love with him. The Black Moment should come when the conflict is at its highest pitch. At that moment, we've got to knock the feet out from under Sally, plunge her into the depths of despair.

I can think of one good way. We can simply have Bill give up his thesis and stop coming to see her. To Sally and the reader, it looks as though she has lost him. She hasn't, of course, or the story would be over then and there, and on a very dismal note. She must get him back. But how? She can't go crawling to him. Neither can they meet accidentally and make up. Where's the drama and story in that? We have to think of a better and more plausible way.

There *is* a way, and a good one. We have another story line in Sally's struggle to raise her children properly, as a parent would. We can use that story line to solve her love problem. When she found the cannon ball, she assumed her brother had stolen it and, meaning to lecture him later, she had returned it to the campus. Soon after she learns that she will never see Bill again, her brother comes grouching from his room demanding, "Who swiped my cannon ball?" Sally asks sharply, "Who swiped what from whom?" Her brother is quick to defend himself. He says, "I didn't swipe it from anybody. I swapped it with Don, down the street. It was his grandfather's. I gave him an old pair of busted skates for it."

We not only knock the feet out from under Sally, we jump on her as well. We give her a double Black Moment. She loses Bill, and she learns she has misjudged her brother. What does she do about her brother? That night she goes to the campus with a paper bag to bring back the cannon ball and right the wrong she has done him. There she meets Bill. Do they make up? Yes, but how? What brings them together? We can't answer that question until we go back and fill in the Middle section of the story and find some angle.

At the end of scene one, remember, we left Sally on the porch, feeling depressed because Bill is not so much interested in her as in her family as a subject for his thesis. At this point, and no later, we have to show Sally struggling with her family problem, so let's take her into the house and put her through some paces that will bring her problem into sharp focus and, at the same time, reveal her as a very sympathetic character. She cooks supper, washes the dishes, puts the kids to bed, beds down Aunt Martha, goes over her budget, then tries to do her homework. But she is so tired, she goes to bed herself.

Now we must bring Bill back into the story. The next day let's have him waiting for her on the steps of the library. He goes with her while she does some grocery shopping and carries her bundles home. He suggests that they all go on a picnic on Sunday, and they all agree. Sunday he picks them up in his rattletrap old car and they go to a lake. The kids sail boats, and Sally and Bill talk.

There's something wrong with our story here. It's going to get repetitious if Bill keeps coming and going from the house. It would be better if we could keep him on scene all the time. Well, why not? Why not have him move in with them? He can't move right into the house with them, so why not have him move into a room over Sally's garage? He suggests it, she agrees, and the scene ends.

But that's a flat scene. Where's the rising and falling action? It isn't there, so we'll have to put it there. But how? There's only one way. The same way we did it in the first scene, only this time intensify it. Sally thinks Bill is interested in her, and again her hopes are

dashed. At the beginning of the picnic, Bill can say nice
things to her, that she's wonderful with the kids, that
she's unquestionably the prettiest girl on the campus.
Then when he proposes moving into her garage, she
realizes (falsely) that he is not interested in her at all
but in his darn thesis. All his pretty speeches and the
nice things he does have been only part of his research.
The action has risen, and fallen once again.

This scene is a good place to have Sally make her un-
fortunate remark about wanting a million dollars. Let's
have Bill ask her what she wants most in the world. She
wants *him,* but she can't say it. Instead she says, "A million dollars." He was about to kiss her, but he pulls
back with a frown. He agrees that a million dollars
would be nice, that it must take a lot to raise a family
these days. He adds with a deeper frown, "More than
most of us have, I guess," meaning himself. Because of
his financial insecurity he holds aloof from her.

To keep the conflict up, let's have Sally very hurt,
and really mad at Bill. When he moves into the garage
the next day, she greets him coldly. For two days she
avoids him, but the third day he catches her in the back
yard and makes her listen to him. He tells her that he is
glad to be her tenant because he likes her and her family. He says that he likes to be near her. For a minute,
Sally believes him, then reason takes over. "In the interests of sociology you tell the most beautiful lies," she
almost tells him, but says instead, "Please let me by."
When she tries to leave, he kisses her. For another moment she thinks she is in heaven, then she remembers,
and pushes him away. "You and your thesis," she cries

and rushes off. She is thoroughly shaken. Once again she was almost blinded by his pretty speeches and, this time, by his kiss. The action has risen to a crisis.

This is the time to hit her with the first Black Moment. When she gets home that night, she finds her children and Aunt Martha in a deep gloom. As we planned earlier, Bill is gone—for good, they tell her. She is stunned, and all her anger and resentment and disappointment leave her, and she suddenly feels as though everything inside of her has become a vacuum. She goes to his room over the garage to see if his leaving is really true. It is. The room's bare. He's gone, all right.

At this point we are dangerously close to having the story fizzle out on us. It isn't enough for him to leave, then in the final scene have them meet again and simply express their love for each other. We need something to carry over from this scene into the next to lead them logically and dramatically into their declarations of love. But what?

Suppose she finds his uncompleted thesis in the waste basket. She takes it out and reads it. It's about her and her family, but he has been very careful to conceal their identity. She finds one page on which is written, "Possible Solution to This Family's Problem"—but the page is blank. He hasn't finished it.

Now we have our bridge over into the end scene. She goes back into the house, and her brother complains that someone has swiped his cannon ball. That night she goes to retrieve it. She meets Bill. She tells him that he has forgotten his thesis. He says he won't be needing it; he's gone back to his original one. When Sally wants to know why, he tells her that there's only one solution, and he can't write about it. Sally wants to know what it is, and he says that the girl in the thesis should fall in love with, and marry, some nice young man capable of supporting her and her family. Because they're talking in the abstract, she asks boldly if he doesn't mean a young assistant sociology professor. He tells her she can do better than that and she wants to know how. She can marry someone with that million dollars, he answers; an assistant professor of sociology makes barely enough money to feed a family of fleas. Sally pauses just long enough to consider her words carefully, then she asks if he doesn't like them any more? He doesn't reply, and he doesn't have to. He looks down at her, and in that moment she knows all she will ever have to know. It's in his face. It's in his eyes. She stands on tiptoe and kisses him. She suddenly knows that Bill has been struggling with a problem of his own, a purely male problem of pride and a sense of inadequacy. It all ends happily with Bill kissing her and proposing marriage.

Your story and your style

There's the complete outline of a story, worked out in detail. But this story is distinctly, and distinctively, *mine*. No other writer, given the same opening situation, would write the same story. Some might have done worse, many would have done better. To this story I gave my own point of view toward life and love, my own individuality, my own style of writing. The story *is* me.

You will do exactly the same thing to your story. You

will give to it *your* style, *your* individuality, *your* viewpoint, *your* attitude toward problems. This makes your story uniquely *yours*.

Nevertheless our stories, yours and mine, will be structurally identical. If two architects were given the same assignment, to build a fifty-unit apartment house, *structurally* they would follow the same basic principles used in the construction of all buildings, but in *design* they would in all probability be totally different. Each would reflect the designers own individuality. In design, therefore, all our stories will be different, but structurally they will be the same. We shall both follow the principles used in the construction of all stories. We will use the formulas and patterns and other elements of technique to bring our stories to dramatic climaxes.

Nor will the structure show, any more than the steel girders of the apartment house show beneath the brick. In writing, this is the mark of the professional. Each story becomes uniquely the author's, but the framework is not obvious to the reader. He has covered it with the brick or, in this case, with his individuality and style. It is something that no one can imitate. It is what makes the very difficult business of writing both fascinating and rewarding.

❧ 11

WHICH VIEWPOINT?

ONE OF THE FIRST THINGS to decide when planning a story is the viewpoint to be used, the one best suited to the material. There are five viewpoints from which a story can be told. Two of these are used quite commonly, the other three only occasionally; but it's a good idea to be familiar with all five of them. You never know when you might want to use them.

The two most commonly used points of view are:
1. The Third Person
2. The First Person

Third-person viewpoint

The *Third-Person Viewpoint* is the most commonly used of all. The author tells his story from the viewpoint of the protagonist, *and from the viewpoint of the protagonist only.* You will find third-person stories in which the viewpoint switches from the protagonist to some other character, but it requires skill and know-how to do this effectively, and even then, at best, the story suffers from it. A switch breaks reader identification with the protagonist; the reader has to make an adjustment and identify himself with a new character; and no matter how well it is done, there is a lag, a drop in interest, in your story. Show your *secondary* character through his dialogue and actions, but *never* through his thinking. *When you go into a secondary character's thinking, you have switched viewpoints.*

When using the protagonist's viewpoint, only you act out or dramatize the story through his actions, dialogue, and thoughts. You stay with him from beginning to end. The story unfolds to the reader *through the protagonist's eyes,* not through the eyes of any other character. We are speaking here, of course, of short stories. In novels the viewpoint is often switched, within chapters, or from chapter to chapter.

Let's give an example of straight third-person viewpoint:

> One slow step at a time Glenn waded through the swamp, Jane holding to his shoulder as she walked beside him in water up to her chest. All around them, the swamp lay wet and dripping after the heavy rain. The moon had broken through the clouds and Glenn could make out the dim shapes of trees, moss-covered and with vines clinging to their branches; and great hummocks of land spaced every fifty or a hundred yards. In between was black water, muddy and evil-smelling.
>
> But now both their steps quickened and a cry of hope sprang to Jane's lips. The water had turned shallow; now, suddenly, they were standing in it up to their thighs. Ahead of them a solid black wall marked the edge of the forest.
>
> The water grew still more shallow. They splashed the last fifty yards and came to dry ground. Jane sank down wearily. "Just let me get my breath," she pleaded.

Studying the forest, Glenn searched his memory. He said: "There's a road that follows the river south from Chickasaw. It skirts the edge of the swamp somewhere near here."

Jane rose to her feet instantly. He tried to push her back, but she said insistently, "No, I'm all right." She clung to his arm. "It's late, and Chickasaw's a long ways from here."

This passage is dramatized through Glenn's (the protagonist's) eyes. "Glenn could make out the dim shape of trees." "Studying the forest." "Glenn searched his memory." At no time did we go into Jane's thoughts. Now let's take the same scene and switch to Jane's viewpoint to illustrate what we mean by *switching viewpoints*. Let's put the "switches" in italics:

One slow step at a time Glenn waded through the swamp, Jane holding to his shoulder as she walked beside him in water up to her chest. *She felt tired, frightened.* All around them the swamp lay wet and dripping after the heavy rain. The moon had broken through the clouds and Glenn could make out the dim shapes of trees, moss-covered and with vines clinging to their branches; and great hummocks of land spaced every fifty or a hundred yards. *In between, Jane saw, was black water, muddy and evil-smelling.* But now both their steps quickened and a cry of hope sprang to Jane's lips. The water had turned shallow; now, suddenly, they were standing in it up to their thighs. Ahead of them a solid black wall marked the edge of the forest. *"Thank heavens," Jane thought, "we're not going to drown after all."*

The water grew still more shallow. They splashed the last fifty yards and came to dry ground. Jane sank down wearily. "Just let me get my breath," she pleaded.

Studying the forest, Glenn searched his memory. He said: "There's a road that follows the river south from

Chickasaw. It skirts the edge of the swamp somewhere near here."

Jane rose to her feet instantly. *She remembered the road, too.* He tried to push her back, but she said insistently, "No, I'm all right. She held to his arm, *afraid she might lose him in the dark.* "It's late, and Chickasaw's a long ways from here."

You can readily see from this last example how interest in the two characters is divided. This is from a novel, and if the whole novel were written in this vein, the result would be confusing.

First-person viewpoint

Now let's take up the *First-Person Viewpoint*, or the "I" viewpoint. It is used frequently, probably because it is the easiest viewpoint from which to tell a story. It eliminates all danger of switching viewpoints because the author automatically stays with the "I" character. The author, through the "I" character, can also say what he wants about any of the secondary characters. It is *his* story. The action, dialogue, and thinking are more *told* than *dramatized*. It takes far less effort to do this.

Here's the same scene as above converted to the first-person viewpoint:

One slow step at a time I waded through the swamp, Jane holding to my shoulder as she walked beside me in water up to her chest. All around us the swamp lay wet and dripping after the heavy rain. The moon had broken through the clouds, and I could make out the dim shapes of trees, moss-covered and with vines clinging to their branches; and great hummocks of land spaced every fifty or a hundred yards. In between was black water, muddy and evil-smelling.

But now both our steps quickened, and a cry of hope sprang to Jane's lips. The water had turned shallow; now, suddenly, we were standing in it up to our thighs. Ahead of us a solid black wall marked the edge of the forest.

The water grew still more shallow. We splashed the last fifty yards and came to dry ground. Jane sank down wearily. "Just let me get my breath," she pleaded.

Studying the forest, I searched my memory. I said: "There's a road that follows the river south from Chickasaw. It skirts the edge of the swamp somewhere near here."

Jane rose to her feet instantly. I tried to push her back, but she said insistently, "No, I'm all right." She clung to my arm. "It's late, and Chickasaw's a long ways from here."

The three less commonly used points of view are:

1. The Objective
2. The Minor Character Narrator
3. The Omniscient

Objective viewpoint

The *Objective Viewpoint* is unique in that the author *never* goes into the minds of any of his characters. It is a completely objective viewpoint. The only way the author has of revealing how the protagonist feels and thinks about a situation is through his reactions, dialogue, and action. This viewpoint is especially useful when the author wants to keep the protagonist's motivation hidden until the end. If he goes into the protagonist's mind for *any* reason, he must also reveal the motivation. Not to do so would be cheating the reader, who would resent this and would stop reading the story.

An example of the viewpoint used to hide motivation is from a story already discussed in this book. The protagonist refuses to let his neighbor dig up his strawberry patch to free a dog that has fallen into an old abandoned well pipe. If the motivation, or reason, for his refusal is revealed at the opening, there will be no suspense, no story. It will end there. So his reason is held back until the end: He desperately needs the money to buy a special bed for his crippled boy. Throughout the story the reader cannot understand the reason for not allowing a small strawberry patch to be dug up to save a dog's life. The reader grows to dislike the protagonist. But when the motivation is revealed this dislike turns to sympathy. Strong emotions are thereby aroused in the reader toward our protagonist.

Here's a short passage from that story:

Dan Clements rose to his feet and said quietly, "There won't be no digging done."

The Wingates, father and son, looked at him in astonishment.

"What're you talking about?" Branch Wingate asked finally.

Dan repeated, "There won't be no digging."

"Why not?"

Dan looked out across his empty fields. "I don't have water for irrigation, and the drought took my crop before the seeds had a chance to sprout." His glance came back to the strawberry patch grimly. "This's all I got left."

Now let's take the same scene and write it subjectively. Let's go into Dan's thoughts and reveal his motivation.

Dan Clements rose to his feet and said quietly, "There won't be no digging done."

The Wingates, father and son, looked at him in astonishment.

"What're you talking about?" Branch Wingate asked finally.

Dan thought of his son, Danny, lying in the house, crippled, and desperately needing a special kind of bed to ease his pain. A bed this strawberry patch would buy. He repeated angrily, "There won't be no digging."

Here we have gone into Dan's thoughts and revealed his motivation for refusing to have his strawberry patch dug up. The story is no longer told objectively. Later in the story, Wingate starts to dig up the patch, and Dan tries to stop him with a shotgun. Still later, at the climax, Dan has a change of heart. He was desperate, but he didn't want to see the dog die either. But by revealing the motivation much of the drama of the story has been lost. The action that follows becomes pointless.

Minor character viewpoint

The *Minor Character Viewpoint* is just what the title implies. The story is told through the minor character's eyes *about* another character who is the real protagonist. Reader identification is established between the reader and the minor character who observes the action and tells the story as an "I" narrator. He may enter into the action in a *minor* way, or he may remain aloof from it. This minor character may also be a group of people, a whole town, a family, or a ship's crew. In such cases, the pronoun "we" is used throughout the story.

The "I" or "we" of the Minor Character Viewpoint should not be confused with the "I" of the First-Person Viewpoint. In the First-Person Viewpoint, the "I" is the narrator and the protagonist or hero. In the Minor Character Viewpoint, the "I" or "we" is only the narrator.

Here's an example of the Minor Character Viewpoint:

> It's a good job, being a trusty and working in the warden's office. It keeps a person eight to twenty-four hours ahead of the grapevine; and it's interesting at times. I'm in for ninety-eight years (seventy still to go), and without this job I'm not sure I could take it.
>
> This one morning was one of the interesting mornings. Jack Ballard was in the warden's office talking to the warden, and the kid was waiting on the bench in the outer office where I have my desk. Ballard was the toughest con in prison and I'd left the door open a crack so I could hear what he had to say, but at the same time I couldn't take my eyes off the kid. He was the youngest convict I'd ever seen. His record said he was *only* fifteen.

In the balance of the story, Ballard is given the job of disciplining the kid, who is incorrigible. The kid is the protagonist, Ballard is a secondary character, and the "I" character is the narrator. The entire story is revealed through the narrator's eyes. He is present in every scene.

Omniscient viewpoint

The *Omniscient Viewpoint* is the hardest of all to write and the one most seldom used. In this viewpoint, the author knows all about all the characters in the story. He knows all and tells all, switching viewpoints whenever he chooses. The chief reasons it is difficult to write a story from this viewpoint are: 1. the switches in viewpoint must be done smoothly, and this requires great skill; and 2. reader identification is never established between the reader and any single character. The story thus may be interesting, but strong emotion is seldom aroused in the reader. And, as we know, the chief reason for writing a story is to arouse an emotional response within the reader.

Here's an example of the Omniscient Viewpoint:

"Why do you two want a divorce?" their lawyer, and best friend, asked.

Bill hesitated. He hated having to drag up all the misery of the past few years. "I think my wife has given you enough reasons," he answered coldly.

Jane breathed a sigh of relief. There were some things she couldn't bear to have Bill tell. Things she was sorry for, and ashamed of.

Here we have gone into the minds of both characters and given their emotional reactions to the lawyer's question. I, as the author, have made use of the Omniscient Viewpoint. In the body of the story the viewpoint is switched from one character to the other at will.

≈ 12

WHAT ABOUT FLASHBACKS?

A FLASHBACK is exactly what the word implies. You're a thousand or so words into your story, say, and you decide you want to introduce an incident that happened prior to your story action. So you *flash back* to this incident. It could be an incident that motivates your main character, or it could be an incident that establishes his dominant character trait. No matter what it is, you plan the incident in scenes. (We'll show how this is done in just a minute.)

Flashbacks fall into two categories:

1. The flashback story
2. The flashback found within the framework of a chronologically told story

Let's take *the flashback story* first. You see it in magazines and on TV all the time. An innocent man is in the death cell with only half an hour to go before his execution. The scene fades, and we pick him up again a year, or ten years, earlier. Three-quarters of the story concerns itself with how and why he got into the death cell when he was innocent. At the end we pick him up again in the death cell where, in the last page or two pages, he gets, or doesn't get, his pardon.

Or, let's say, two men are drifting in a lifeboat in the middle of the Atlantic Ocean. They are near death from thirst and starvation, but it isn't necessary to flash back to find out how they got there. Suppose, however, that one has a knife and is trying to kill the other, that he is accusing the other man of stealing his wife, and the other man is denying it. Now we want to know more about the situation. So we flash back, and in this flashback reveal what has happened between them up until this moment.

This type of story is used primarily to build suspense. And when used properly it can be quite effective.

Now let's take *the flashback found within the framework of a chronologically told story.* This is an entirely different type and may be only a page or so long, and it is used *not to tell the whole story* but merely to bring in some necessary information, or perhaps to reveal the protagonist's motivation. As we have said, this type of flashback is worked out in scenes, is acted out dramatically, not *narrated. When information or motivation is narrated, it is not a flashback at all.*

The trick, of course, is in "getting into" and "getting out of" the flashback smoothly. There are two principal ways of doing this. One is the abrupt cut from past tense to past tense. Let's say that the story has been going on for perhaps a scene or two in the past tense. Then we give our protagonist a chance to pause and think (use a triple space) and plunge right into the

flashback, in *the same tense*. The triple space denotes
the change in time:

> He was walking along the beach when he first met Jane.
> It was ten years ago to the day. He remembered it all so
> vividly.

We are now in the flashback and what happened that
day, and perhaps in succeeding days, is presented in
scenes.

The second way is a smoother approach. *The pluperfect tense* is used for a paragraph or two, then the author drops back into *the past tense* and acts out the
scene. As in the first example, let's say that the story has
been going on for a scene or two in the past tense. Then
again we give our protagonist a chance to pause and
think. Now here we go into the flashback:

> He had been walking along the beach when he'd first
> met Jane. It had been ten years ago to the day. They'd
> started to pass each other; then on an impulse he'd
> spoken to her.
> "Hi," he said.
> Her glance lifted to his uncertainly, hesitantly. "Hello,"
> she answered, and started to walk on hurriedly.

The same methods are used for "coming out" of a
flashback. Triple space and abruptly cut from past tense
to past tense; or use the pluperfect again for a paragraph
or two, to accent the jump in time. For example:

The abrupt cut:

> And that was the way it was the first time they met.
> Everything wonderful. Everything so right. And now?

By the use of the pluperfect:

That first day had been the best day of their lives. They'd met; they'd become friends; they'd started to become lovers. But now?

Now he looked down at her sleeping beside him and he thought, "What a witch she is." But almost in the same breath he thought, "And what a bum I am."

Now, in order that you fully understand this latter method, let's give a longer version:

Lisa turned away from her husband, Bill, and stared incredulously at the shabbily dressed man standing before her. She couldn't believe it. She sank slowly to the sofa, a feeling of apprehension welling up inside of her. It couldn't be. It just couldn't be her father after all these years. (Now we go into the flashback, in the pluperfect tense.)

She'd been only eight years old the last time she'd seen him. He and her mother had had a terrible fight and he'd walked out. He'd left her mother lying on the bed, crying. (Now we switch into the *past* tense.)

"Did daddy hurt you, mommy?" Lisa stood there, a small frown on her brow.

"Please, Lisa. Please, don't."

"But, mommy—"

"Lisa, please." Her mother turned away, as though trying to hide her tears. "You're too young to understand."

The body of the flashback scene follows. Then we start to "come out" of it.

That night at the supper table Lisa glanced up at her mother, the small frown on her brow deeper. "Isn't daddy going to eat with us tonight?"

"I don't know." Her mother stared helplessly at her plate. "I really don't know," she whispered.

Lisa's blue eyes darkened. "I guess daddy doesn't love us any more," she said. "Maybe he ran away, mommy. Maybe he won't ever come back."

"Stop it, Lisa." It burst from her mother's lips. "Stop it." (Now we go into the *pluperfect* tense again.)

She'd finished her supper that night and had crept into bed. All night she'd waited for the knob to turn, for the door to slam. But her father hadn't come back that night, or any night, ever. It had been twenty years now since she'd seen him. Twenty long years since he'd walked out of the house. (And now we go back into the *past* tense, and into the main body of the story again.)

Lisa glanced warily at her husband and then sank deeper into the sofa. She stared even harder at the man. But there was no resemblance—not a trace of similarity of any kind. Suddenly all the bitterness inside of her rose to the surface.

"You're not my father," she cried. "You're an impostor." Her voice rose sharply. "Get out! Get out of this house at once!"

A flashback in a chronologically told story should be introduced in the *beginning* section of your story, or at the beginning of the *middle* section, *but no later*. To bring material of this kind in later is as disrupting as introducing a major character three quarters of the way through your story.

Flashbacks are commonly used, but I, personally, try to avoid them. I prefer to tell a story chronologically and feed in any flashback material through dialogue, through the protagonist's thoughts, or through short passages of narration. In this way the action is not stopped; a story has better unity; it is not broken up.

Here are some illustrations of feeding flashback material into a story:

When Bill's gaze returned to the picture of Sally, the feeling of irritation melted. It vanished altogether, like an evil thing, and he sighed. That was what Sally did to him.

That was what Sally had been doing to him ever since he'd laid eyes on her in the studio when, during a single hour's broadcast, he'd first come under her spell.

Bill got up and walked into the sitting room for a cigarette. Their engagement had caused a small furor amongst his friends. "Not the queen and the country boy! Not good old conscientious Bill! Not the Squire of Seventy-Second Street!" They couldn't believe it; he and Sally were such opposites.

"Lucky stiff," they'd said too. And he knew he was. To be married to a girl like Sally was something ninety-nine percent of the male population could only dream about.

Many beginning writers would have set the scene of the meeting between Bill and Sally in the studio, having the couple get to know each other and then throw a party to announce their engagement. How much better, and easier, it is to do it this way, in three short paragraphs. Here's another example:

His father's letter had been a plea for help. After the harsh words they had had, after the bitter scene that had led to his leaving home four years ago, his father had had enough stubborn pride not to ask for help outright. But the plea had been there between the lines. Glenn's reply had been to take the next boat downriver.

He wanted to see his father again; wanted to go home again for a visit. He had received only two communications from his father in four years. The other had told him of his mother's death and had reached him two months before when he was four hundred miles up the Missouri on a fur-trading expedition and couldn't do anything about it. The letter had been brief, without particulars. Its shortness had angered him at first, then made him wonder if his father were holding back some information. It had given him a sense of uneasiness he hadn't been able to shake off.

Here again the beginner might have put into a flashback the fight between Glenn and his father; or the scene when Glenn receives his father's letter. Later on in this story the reason for the fight between father and son is brought out in a brief passage of dialogue:

> "You've been away a long time," his father said, "and I'd like to have you home now." He kept his back turned and after a moment's hesitation he added gruffly, "I've missed you."
>
> Glenn closed his portmanteau and snapped the lock. At the sound his father spun quickly and faced him.
>
> "I know what you've been thinking." His voice was harsh. "I have no right to ask you. You can't believe that I've missed you."
>
> Glenn hesitated. "I'm afraid I've already made other arrangements."
>
> His father's mouth twisted painfully. "Ones that can't be changed?"
>
> "I've promised my help in a venture to the Western Territory."
>
> Disappointment etched deeper lines into his father's face. He drew a long, full breath. "We won't talk about it any more now." He paused. "But I hope you'll see your way clear to changing your mind, to stop this wandering life of yours."

Instead of showing the fight or quarrel between Glenn and his father, the author has fed the information into the story unobtrusively. It has not stopped the story action.

✒ 13

CHECK LIST: HOW TO MAKE EDITORS READ WHAT YOU WRITE

EDITORS ARE eager and anxious to find a good story! This statement is a little difficult to believe sometimes. When I started writing, I didn't believe it. I thought all editors were hard-hearted and that they took delight, not only in returning manuscripts, but in enclosing the bluntest rejection slips they could devise.

But a few years later, when I became an editor myself, I found out how wrong my thinking had been. The editor is definitely eager and anxious to find a good story. The very life of his magazine, and therefore his job, depends on it. The same goes for the editorial reader who sees your script first. Many a reader has received a fat bonus, or a promotion to assistant editor, for discovering a new and promising writer.

Some magazines receive thousands of scripts a month. Their staffs aren't big enough, however, to read these scripts all the way through. The procedure in some offices is to read the first page or two, a middle page or two, and the last page. This gives a trained reader a pretty good idea of whether or not the script has merit. If it hasn't, back it goes to you, accompanied by one of those hateful rejection slips. If it *has* merit, then he reads your script all the way through, carefully.

How do you make the editor read your script all the way through? You must arouse and hold his interest, from the first word to the last. To help you make certain that your story will do this, a Check List of what should be in your story to make it salable is presented here. Some of these points have been discussed elsewhere in this book and are repeated here, though not in detail.

Here's the Check List presented with a few comments:

1. Is your story material important?

For years I wrote stories about my family, my neighbors, my friends, my cats, my dogs. All of these subjects were potentially important story material, but I didn't make good use of them, didn't make them important or of interest to anyone but myself. I was a please-myself writer, not a please-the-editor-and-his-millions-of-readers writer. For example, I once wrote a story about my dog and how I served as midwife when she was having puppies. It was merely a humorous account of my efforts to be helpful. It interested me, but failed to interest an editor. Years later I took this same situation and reworked it. I made my protagonist a boy whose mother had just died in childbirth. The boy can't understand why his mother had to die; he suspects his baby brother is somehow to blame. His grief and resentment are so intense, he hits the baby. He resents his father, too, because of his concern over the baby. That is one of the story problems. Running parallel to it is another about the boy's dog having puppies. The mother dog dies giving birth to an overly large litter. The puppies' father tries helplessly to care for the pups. The boy's father at this point gently points out to his son that birth and death are not controlled by man, but by a higher power. He also explains that the father dog's concern for the puppies is no different from his own for the baby, that it is concern and love for the weak and helpless and doesn't in any way alter his love for his other son. With the facts explained at a level the boy can understand, the boy "comes to realize" the truth in what his father tells him.

Unimportant story material in this case was made important by utilizing one of the great experiences of life, death; and two of the basic human emotions, love and hate. Marriage, life, death, adventure, love, are basically important. Mistakes, quarrels, misunderstandings that can be cleared up by the author at any time with a few words, are unimportant. The first thing a writer should do when he gets an idea for a story is to ask himself: Is this material important, and if it isn't, can it be made important? If the answer to these questions is in the negative, he should forget the story and think up another.

2. What is the theme?

It is difficult to find a published short story that hasn't some kind of theme. Sometimes it's there by chance; most of the time it's there by design. If the author is conscious of the theme, the writing is easier, because theme gives a story direction and unity. Theme is the statement of a basic truth. "Kindness brings its own rewards." "Honesty is the best policy." "God helps those who help themselves." Theme should be implied, never stated in your story, never preached. One of the things to do before starting a story is to sit down and write out your theme in one sentence. This clarifies it in your mind and, when you know what you are trying to say, you are able to steer your story through to a satisfying conclusion.

3. Do you have a catchy title?

When an editor picks up your story the first thing he sees is the title. If it is dull, flat, uninteresting, he subconsciously expects a dull, flat, uninteresting story, and you have one strike against you before he even starts reading. On the other hand, if the title is intriguing, if it interests him, you are on your way to first base. Suppose you title your story, "Blue Skies Over Miami." So what? the editor asks himself. Why shouldn't they be blue? But suppose you use the title, "Red Skies Over Miami." Now you have posed the question, why red? Blood is red. Fire is red. Is there fighting of some kind going on in Miami? Or is it burning? The editor is curious to know what is happening. His interest whetted, he starts reading.

Take the title, "Call Off the Wedding." Whose wedding, the editor wonders; and why call it off? Take "The Outcasts." What outcasts? Why are they outcasts? Again the editor's interest has been aroused. But use "Wet Pavements," or "My Aunt Gladys," for titles, and you have dulled his interest, perhaps fatally.

How does one think up good titles? The title should tie in somehow with the story. Perhaps a line from the story itself will suffice. Perhaps the theme can be implied, but not stated directly. Sometimes the setting, if unusual, can be incorporated. When I'm stuck for a title, I usually resort to *Bartlett's Familiar Quotations* (a paperback edition can be bought at any big newsstand), or the Bible, or any good book of poetry. I never send a story out until I am satisfied with the title, even if it takes me a month to find the right one.

4. Have you chosen the most effective viewpoint?

This subject has been discussed fully in a previous chapter. Suffice it to repeat here that you'll often find that a story will become a better story when told from the viewpoint of a character different from the one originally planned. The point to keep in mind is simply that the viewpoint character to choose is the one most emotionally affected by the problem.

5. Are you beginning as close to the climax as you can?

Many unpublished manuscripts remain unpublished because the authors take too long to get their stories going. They start too far back, too far away from the *problem*'s start. If you're writing a story of a couple's divorce, do not begin at their wedding, or the day they first met, or were born. The problem is divorce, so get on with it. "I want a divorce," he said—and you have your problem stated and your characters in conflict. You're about ten years into your character's lives and twelve hundred or so unimportant words nearer your climax. If your problem has not been stated in the first page or page and a half, you'd better examine your outline carefully. Past information can be woven into the story later on, through thoughts or straight narrative telling, and detailed setting and characterization can be held back until later. The main thing is to get your *story* going so your reader will have something to interest him and keep him reading. Your job as a writer is to interest your reader emotionally in characters in conflict over a problem. Doing this as close to the climax as possible will give you a far tighter and more dramatic story.

6. What motivates your main characters?

Lack of motivation is one of the chief reasons for a story being "slight." Strong motivation gives a story depth. Why do your characters act the way they do? This question must be answered fully before you start to write. A man is crazy for money—perhaps he had a desperately poor early life. A young girl keeps turning down proposals—she is still tied to her mother's apron strings. Motivation helps make your characters real and plausible. *They become people acting with reason.*

7. Do you have two story lines?

For years I wrote stories along a straight action line and collected only rejection slips. Then one day an editor wrote and suggested I add a character line, or character problem. I did this on my next story and it promptly sold. A character problem is a character weakness or strength in your protagonist. The two problems, action and character, parallel each other throughout the story, and one helps to resolve the other at the climax. Your story now has depth; and your protagonist is a rounder and more real character.

8. Does your first page have the Seven Points for Story Beginnings? (This is covered in detail in Chapter 2.)

9. Is your story new and fresh?

New and unusual settings and characters will arouse immediate interest in the editor. In one story, I had my protagonist, as you'll remember, raising vegetables on his penthouse terrace. There is nothing new or unusual about a New York penthouse, but add a vegetable garden, and it becomes an unusual setting. Furthermore it takes a rather unusual person to think of raising vegetables six or seven hundred feet up in the air. Both the setting and the character aroused the editor's interest in the story.

There was a time when space travel was an unusual subject; today it is commonplace. But if a man undertakes to drill down into the earth's core and convert its heat energy to industrial use, this is unusual and interesting. Faraway places are new and interesting if they haven't been written to death already. An unusual character would be one that varies from the norm. This doesn't mean he should be an odd-ball. Readers of fiction like to identify themselves with the protagonist, and if he is too weird, they are unable to. If you are using an unusual character, he should have all the traits of a recognizable and identifiable person.

10. Are the beginning, middle and end properly proportioned?

There is no set rule on this. Approximately, in a sixteen-page story, you can allot four pages to the beginning, ten or eleven to the middle, one or one and a half to the end. By the end of the fourth page you have the problem fully stated and the protagonist starting out to resolve this problem. You are now in the middle part of your story which continues to the climax. What follows the climax is the end.

11. Does your story action rise and fall?

A bad story starts on a certain emotional level and plods through to the conclusion without ever deviating from it. In a good story, the emotional level never remains static; that is, it never goes in a straight line. It rises and falls. It rises when your protagonist approaches a crisis in his effort to solve his problem. It falls when his effort fails. It starts to rise again when he makes a second effort, falls when this second attempt also fails. This rising and falling action holds the editor's interest. Without it your story becomes monotonous and boring.

Another good way to lose the editor's interest is to run the action and emotion straight uphill for four or five thousand words. You can do this by eliminating all falling action. The protagonist starts to solve his problem, reaches a crisis, hurdles it, tears on to the second without thought or a reaction of any sort, hurdles the second, and the third, and the fourth. I used to do this, until an editor wrote me one day saying, "Your story left me out of breath but with enough strength left to mail it back to you." I got his message all right, and the next story I sent him had plenty of rising and falling action in it. And it sold.

12. Is there suspense in your story?

Suspense in a story is aroused by confronting the protagonist with obstacles so strong that grave doubts are raised over whether or not he will succeed in his struggle. Weak obstacles make for weak suspense. An obstacle should rock the protagonist back on his heels. It should overwhelm him, lick him momentarily. Only at the climax of the story should he triumph. The rougher you make his struggle, the stronger will be your suspense.

Another way to arouse suspense is to foreshadow, or give a promise of, danger or heightened conflict to come. A simple example of this would be for the villain to threaten the protagonist or someone the protagonist loves. The editor's interest will be aroused, and he will read on to see if the threat is carried out and, if it is, how the protagonist will meet it. The technique of foreshadowing is seldom used by beginners, but it is an excellent way of creating suspense.

13. Do you have contrast in your story?

Not so long ago a friend brought me a story to criticize. His protagonist's name was Ben Ragan. His villain's name was Lem Dugan. There was little contrast in names, and it was easy to confuse one character with the other. We changed the villain's name to Nick Slade. Now there *was* contrast. Nick Slade was also a more appropriate name for a villain. In this same story, the protagonist was a big, husky fellow. But so was the villain. For the sake of contrast, we changed Nick Slade to a thin, slight man and, to compensate for his lack of physical strength, made him an expert knife wielder. Characters in your story should be as unlike each other in appearance and name as you can make them. You should not give them the same character traits either. If they are too similar, there will be no clash, the conflict will be weak.

14. Have you used action, instead of inactive, verbs?

A student in one of my classes was having great difficulty with her writing. Her stories were flat and insipid. There was no life to them. I suggested she take one of her stories and count the number of action verbs in it. She did, and found only five. The other verbs, some fifty or sixty in number, were inactive—was, went, had. I then suggested she change these passive verbs to action verbs, and she did so. Her story immediately took on life; it began to *move*. Instead of writing, "He was a tall, blond man. He went out of the room," she wrote, "He strode from the room, ducking his blond head so he wouldn't hit it against the door lintel." Here "strode," and "ducking," and "hit" have been substituted for "was" and "went," and a picture of a character in action has been created. Try combing the passive verbs out of your scripts, and you'll have better, more colorful stories; and they'll be *dramatized*, rather than *told*.

15. Is the dark moment black enough?

There comes a time, just before the climax, when your protagonist's efforts to resolve his problem seem hopeless. The more helpless they seem, the stronger will be your climax and, therefore, the more dramatic your story. Many beginning writers back away from getting their heroes into too much trouble, because they're afraid they can't get them out of it. They can. They can plant their way out. It is also true that the blacker the black moment, the more readily the reader will accept a solution.

16. Does your story reach a dramatic climax?

This has been covered in the chapter on plot, but

it may be well to repeat here that your story *will* reach a dramatic climax if the proper sequence is followed in presenting the various elements leading *up to* the climax. Then you can't fail.

17. Have you violated any taboos?

What can't you write about; what taboos are there? In novel writing there aren't many left. The reputable magazine publishers are more strict, however. They will consider stories on almost any subject, but they must be presented in *good taste*. How does one write a story about homosexuality, for instance, in good taste? By *implication,* rather than by *detailed action*. The emphasis is not on the act of homosexuality, but on how homosexuality affects the lives of the characters in the story.

18. Is your story trite?

Have you ever had a manuscript come back from a publisher with the comment, "This story is trite." By trite the editor simply means, "This story has been done a thousand, or ten thousand, times before." Wait a minute, you say; how about the Cinderella story; that's been done a thousand times, is trite, and is still being done. Yes, it is. But when you read it in a magazine, or see it on TV, something usually has been added. It's the same old story, and still a very popular one, but it has been made new and fresh in some way. The freshness, perhaps, is in the characterization, or in setting, or in approaching the problem from a new angle. But fresh and new it must be to get by.

Triteness is also found in the *writing* in many stories, in the similes, metaphors, etc. For example, "Green as grass," is trite. But, "Green as the envy in Jane's eyes," is fresher. It not only emphasizes the word "green"; it characterizes Jane. It serves a double purpose, and takes the triteness, the sameness, out of it. Just remember that triteness is the mark of the amateur; freshness the mark of the professional. The first draft of many professional stories is full of trite phrases, and much of the time and effort spent on rewriting goes toward freshening them up.

19. Have you done enough research on your story?

If you're writing from your own experiences, emotional or factual, you won't need to do much research. But if you're writing about something unfamiliar, either contemporary or historical, you will have to do some studying. Thoroughly familiarize yourself with the subject you're writing about. You may not use even half of what you've learned, but having it at your finger tips will give you the confidence to speak with authority, and the reader will respect you for your knowledge. And, too, in researching a story, the chances are you'll find enough material in characters, situations, conflicts, etc., for a dozen stories. This makes the job not only interesting, but exciting.

That's the whole list. Try using it and see if it doesn't help you. It also can be used advantageously after the first draft of the story is finished and before the rewriting begins.